The Plant-Based Air Fryer Cookbook

Unleash the Art of Delicious Plant-Based Cooking with Effortless Air-Fried Delights. Including a Comprehensive 28-Day Meal Plan for Healthy, Flavorful Living

Written By:

Journey Mallin

Table of Contents

Introduction

Trying an entirely novel diet might be exciting, but it can also be worrisome. You will need to change or adjust some of the components of your current meals. Adopting a new diet can occasionally be as challenging as buying new ingredients and organizing your entire kitchen cabinet, or it can be as simple as buying only one or 2 things.

The human body mainly relies on fat and carbohydrates when it comes to getting the energy required to function during the day. The plant-based air fryer diet is interesting since it might promote faster fat burning in the body. Scientists have long noted that fat is the single substance responsible for weight gain that is linked to a number of illnesses, such as diabetes, obesity, and childhood epilepsy.

Along with the components, how you prepare your food also counts. You may make all of your favorite meals with air fryers in an entirely healthy way. Are you enquiring? An essential kitchen appliance, an air fryer will ensure that food is cooked through hot air circulation inside the chamber. A motorized fan circulates the hot air in the air fryer quickly throughout the food. Instead of requiring gallons of oil, an air fryer simply requires a few drops. Unquestionably, the main benefit of an air fryer is that it requires little to no oil to cook. Since premium fat is so expensive, this benefit alone makes utilizing an air fryer more appealing than using a deep fryer. Additionally, even if you eliminate carbohydrates from your diet, you might still get the crisp texture of your dish. However, refined carbs are not necessary for food to become crispy. All you need is an air fryer and this cookbook. You'll find 200 great vegan dishes in this cookbook and a 28-day food plan. This cookbook makes everything possible: breakfasts, lunches, dinners and sweets, always with a little creativity. Now let's show you what an air fryer can do to support a plant-based diet. Enjoy the journey.

Chapter 1:
Plant-Based and Vegan Diet

1.1 What Is Plant-Based Eating?

A wide range of eating habits falls under the umbrella of plant-based eating, from being vegan (not consuming any animal products) to incorporating minimal to moderate amounts of animal-based foods into your diet.

- You are engaging in a plant-based diet when you eat predominantly items that come from plants, such as vegetables, fruit, whole grains, seeds, beans, legumes, and oils.
- This eating pattern may include trace amounts of animal products, such as meat, fish, seafood, eggs, and dairy.
- Foods and drinks that have no animal ingredients are additionally referred to as being "plant-based," including soy milk and "meat substitutes" (which are often made from soy, modified vegetable protein, and wheat gluten).

Typically, the term "plant-based" only relates to one's diet.

The phrase "plant-based" is frequently used to describe diets that are fully or primarily composed of plant foods. However, some individuals may identify as plant-based while continuing to consume some foods with animal origins.

Others refer to their diet as "whole foods, plant-based" and define it as mostly consisting of entire plant foods that are either raw or little processed.

Unlike vegan or other plant-based diets, people who follow a whole-food, plant-based diet will also avoid processed grains and oils.

Given the prevalence of processed vegan meals, the phrase "whole foods" makes a crucial contrast. A whole food, plant-based diet would not allow for vegan goods like some versions of boxed mac and cheese, hot dogs, cheese slices, bacon, or even "chicken" nuggets.

1.2 What Is Vegan Diet?

Being vegan encompasses more than just a person's diet; it also refers to the way of life that person chooses to live every day. Living in a way that avoids using, consuming, or exploiting animals as much as is practically possible is known as veganism. Although there is still room for personal preferences and restrictions, the primary goal is to ensure that animals suffer as little as possible due to lifestyle decisions. People who identify themselves as vegans usually avoid buying products created with animal products or tested on animals. This frequently includes apparel, toiletries, footwear, accessories, and home items. For some vegans, this may also mean avoiding vaccines or treatments that contain animal by-products or have been tested on animals.

Many people adopt a vegan diet because of strong ethical convictions about animal welfare, environmental concerns, and health. A vegan diet is a plant-based lifestyle that forbids the consumption of animal products. Committed vegans are also against using any goods that have been experimented on animals or wearing leather or wool.

1.3 Difference Between a Vegan Diet and a Plant-Based Diet?

People are deciding to reduce or eliminate their consumption of animal products from their diets. As a consequence, there are now noticeably more alternatives made from plants available at grocery stores, restaurants, gathering places, and fast food establishments. While some use the word "plant-based," others prefer the term "vegan" to describe their way of life. As a result, you may wonder how the 2 names differ from each other. The phrases "vegan" and "plant-based" are compared and contrasted in this article with regard to diet and way of life.

1.4 Veganism Pros and Cons

Vegetarian or vegan diets are more common than ever, especially among athletes looking to improve performance.

A plant-based diet has many advantages and is considered the healthiest because it emphasizes plant-based foods (such as fruits, vegetables, legumes or whole grains).

This is excellent and the ideal state for all diets, but are there any drawbacks to a plant-based diet? For the record, I have nothing against a vegan diet. I only want to make clear any possible dangers and assist all athletes who choose to follow a plant-based diet in achieving the greatest outcomes.

Pros

- Eat a variety of fruits and vegetables every day.
- Useful diet for losing weight
- Higher satiety levels (large food quantity, low energy intake)
- High fiber intake
- Non-vegans won't have any trouble getting their daily needs of protein.

- Normally carbohydrate-rich diets to assist in endurance training

Cons

- Protein and fat levels in vegan meals can be low.
- Vegetarianism may result in frequent nutrient shortages.
- Vegans have more difficulty meeting their requirement for protein without using supplements.
- Increased protein intakes are suggested during dieting, especially for athletes, to encourage muscle retention and recovery, fight hunger, and improve mood.
- As a result, vegans require extra protein because their diets tend to be lower in protein quality than those of vegetarians and meat eaters.

Other Pros and Cons of Veganism

Other notable advantages and disadvantages of being vegan exist besides the ones already covered. Let's discover them:

- **Reduces the risk of heart and cardiovascular disease:** Your diet is one of the major risk factors for heart disease. The vegan diet prioritizes a variety of organic, nutrient-rich plant-based foods that support heart health. All whole grains, produce, legumes, nuts, seeds, and other foods are very healthy.
- According to a study including 126 omnivorous men and 170 vegetarians, vegetarian people tend to have lower blood pressure and a lower risk of developing coronary heart disease.
- **Blood sugar levels are improved:** diabetes of type 2 is a major global health problem. However, some research indicates that a vegan diet specifically helps to lower blood sugar levels. Usually, it lessens the intake of low-quality processed foods, which are excessively consumed in typical Western diets and raise the risk of type 2 diabetes.
- **Potential nutritional deficiency:** A vegan diet may be deficient in some essential elements like protein, vitamin B12, omega-3 fatty acids, zinc, and iron that the body needs to function.

To successfully follow a vegan diet, you must be aware of the essential foods that should be prioritized and combined to meet these nutrient intakes. You also need to analyze your diet (possibly with the assistance of a registered dietitian or nutritionist) to determine whether you need to take any additional supplements to avoid nutrient deficiencies if you find it difficult to get all the nutrients you need from food alone.

1.5 Common Nutrient Deficiencies on a Vegan Diet

Although vegan and vegetarian diets are unquestionably good for your health, removing all animal products from your diet may leave you with several common nutritional shortages.

The following are the most typical dietary inadequacies in vegan and vegetarian diets:

- (Both should take supplements) Vitamin B12
- Everyone should take a vitamin D3 supplement.
- Calcium (the only problem for non-dairy customers is that plant sources may restrict absorption)
- Iron (rich in iron, although absorption may be a problem; incorporate foods and/or supplements high in vitamin C with meals; all vegetarians and vegans; female endurance athletes at high risk of anemia)
- Zinc (a possible issue for vegans)
- Iodine (a possible issue for those who avoid seafood, dairy, and eggs)
- Non-fish eaters must supplement with EPA/DHA derived from algae for omega-3.

Now let's look up vegan alternatives for the deficiencies indicated above:

Calcium sources for vegans

- Veggies with dark leaves, such as broccoli, kale, and cabbage.
- Tofu.
- Milk, bread, and cereals enriched with calcium.
- Stale fruit.
- Hummus and sesame seeds.

Ways to get vitamin D for vegans

- Exposure to direct sunshine.
- Breakfast cereals, soy beverages without added sugar, and fat spreads fortified.
- Supplements with vitamin D3.

Sources of iron for vegans

- Pulses.
- Whole meal flour and bread.
- Cereals for breakfast are iron-fortified. Leafy vegetables that are a dark green color, such as watercress, broccoli, and spring greens.
- Nuts.
- Dried fruit varieties, including figs, prunes, and apricots.

Ways to get vitamin B12 for vegans

- Cereals for breakfast with added B12.
- Drinks made from unsweetened soy that have vitamin B12 added.
- Marmite is a yeast extract that has been fortified alongside vitamin B12.

Omega-3 fatty acids from vegan sources

- Flaxseeds and walnuts.
- Tofu.
- Omega 3 vegan supplement.

1.6 The Five Food Groups of a Plant-Based Diet

What can you even eat, then?

I'm sure the majority of vegans and plant-based eaters are quite familiar with this query. It seems that when you eliminate meat, dairy, eggs and fish from your diet, all you have left is lettuce. But in reality, for most people, a plant-based diet opens up entirely new possibilities for eating a wide variety of delicious dishes!

In order to acquire all of the vitamins, minerals, and additional nutrients our bodies require to feel and operate their best when following a plant-based diet, it's vital to adopt a balanced approach to food and consumer foods from a number of various sources and food categories. On a plant-based diet, it's easy to acquire everything you need, but the trick is to include a variety of foods and enough of them.

When it comes to restricting particular food groups, eating solely from 1 or 2 of them, and not eating enough of any of them, I've been there and done that. It is unsuccessful. And it's the primary reason, in my opinion, why some individuals claim that a vegan diet "doesn't work" for them.

Humans were physiologically designed to eat vegetables. Since we are all members of the same species, a large body of research and other evidence demonstrate that plant-based diets are nutritionally sufficient and effective at preventing, treating, and even curing practically all serious chronic illnesses. Plant-based diets support optimum energy levels, healthy skin, hair, and nails, balanced hormones, healthy weight control without restriction, and much more!

Your age, gender, activity level, objectives, height, and other factors will all affect the quantity of each food group you need to feel and run at your best. However, the 5 plant-based categories of food that make up a good, balanced diet are listed below:

Vegetables

We all know the health benefits of vegetables. They contain a wide variety of vitamins, minerals, phytochemicals, fiber, antioxidants (which are only present in plants and protect us from disease and cell damage!), and other nutrients. On your plate, try adding as many different hues as possible, as every hue often represents a specific vitamin or health benefit that a vegetable may contain.

Even while most veggies are low in energy and highly nutrient-dense, they are nevertheless an excellent method of bulking up your meals while keeping you full. But it's also essential to ensure you're not just eating healthy foods while obtaining enough energy.

Fruits

Contrary to popular opinion, fruit doesn't merely have sugar in it. Fruits have sugar, but it also has a multitude of phytochemicals, minerals, vitamins, and fiber (just like vegetables!) that assist in controlling the absorption of sugar into the circulatory system, offer us power, and have a variety of other amazing health benefits. According to some studies, even twenty servings of fruit a day are good for your health! Fruit is naturally sweet and tasty, making it the perfect snack and the ideal substitute for sugar for breakfasts, cooking, desserts, smoothies, and more. Fruit tastes and is best digested when it is in season and ripe.

Whole Grains

Grains are a great source of complex carbohydrates that digest slowly and help to keep blood sugar and energy levels stable. Whole grains are always preferable to processed grains since they include much more fiber, vitamins, minerals, protein, and vital lipids. Whole grains make an excellent foundation for main dishes when cooked whole. Additionally, they can be ground into flour in baking.

Some of the grains I enjoy are oats, wheat, spelt, wheat, rice, rye, millet, buckwheat, and quinoa (the 3 others are actually seeds or "pseudo-grains," yet we'll include them in this section nevertheless!).

Legumes

Legumes are one food category that is severely underappreciated in our society. The wonderful plant protein, fiber, vitamins, and minerals found in beans, lentils, and other legumes have been linked to a host of health advantages, including the prevention and treatment of chronic disease, control of blood sugar levels, promotion of healthy gut bacteria, and more! They are filling, adaptable, delicious, hearty, and incredibly affordable. Plant energy! I enjoy preparing bean chili, Dahl, curries, and lentil Bolognese and using legumes to make dips like hummus and refried beans. Additionally, they taste fantastic when added to salads or turned into sweet delicacies like black bean brownies, blondes, or cookies. Even though they have undergone a little more processing, soy products like tofu and tempeh are still wonderfully healthy.

Nuts and Seeds

Nutrient and energy powerhouses, nuts and seeds are abundant in vitamins, minerals, fiber, protein, and vital fatty acids. Numerous nuts and seeds include omega-3 fatty acids, which have anti-inflammatory properties and are particularly crucial for hormone, skin, and brain health. Additionally, nuts and seeds provide a lot of flavor and satisfaction to meals. They also make excellent snacks and may be transformed into various dishes, including kinds of nut milk and cheeses, raw cheesecakes, kinds of nut and seed butter, and more.

Chapter 2:
Recipes for Breakfast and Brunch

2.1 Breakfast Cornbread

Preparation Time: 13 min

Cooking Time: 13 min

Servings: 3

Ingredients

- 1 tbsp flaxseed meal
- 2 tbsp water
- 1/2 cup pecans, chopped
- 1/2 cup white cornmeal
- 1/2 cup all-purpose white flour
- 2 tsp baking powder
- 1/2 tsp salt
- 2 tbsp vegetable oil
- 1/2 cup almond milk
- 2 tbsp molasses

For serving:

- Maple syrup

Instructions

Set the air fryer's temperature to 390°F. Combine flaxseed meal and water in a medium bowl and set aside. Cook the toasted walnuts for 2–3 minutes in the pan of the air fryer. Remove from pan and set aside. Combine cornmeal, flour, baking soda, and salt in a large bowl. Combine the oil, milk, and molasses with the flaxseed mixture before adding it. After adding the wet components, integrate the dry ingredients well. Cook for 12–13 minutes, or until a toothpick inserted in the center comes out clean, after pouring the mixture onto the air fryer baking sheet. Remove from the air fryer and let cool for 5 minutes in the pan. Cut 4 slices of bread diagonally. Serve warm, topped with golden walnuts and maple syrup.

Nutritional facts

Calories: 224, Carbohydrates: 32 g, Fat: 8 g, Protein: 5 g

2.2 Donut Bites

Preparation Time: 10 min

Cooking Time: 5 min

Servings: 4

Ingredients

- 1 tbsp Bob's Red Mill egg replacer
- 2 tbsp water
- 1 cup all-purpose white flour
- 4 tbsp coconut sugar, divided
- 1 tsp baking powder
- 1/4 tsp baking soda
- 1/8 teaspoon salt
- 4 oz soft silken tofu
- 1 tsp pure vanilla extract
- 1 tbsp liquid vegan butter
- Cooking spray

Instructions

Set the air fryer's temperature to 390°F before using. Stir together the water and egg replacement in a medium bowl. Mix the flour, 2 tablespoons of sugar, baking powder, baking soda, and salt in a sizable bowl. Add the tofu and vanilla to the egg mixture. With a fork or whisk, break up the tofu and mix until smooth. Add the heated vegan butter and stir. Mix thoroughly after adding the tofu mixture to the dry ingredients. The dough could seem brittle and dry. When you have a stiff dough that holds together, knead the dry crumbs into the mixture using the back of a spoon. Make 16 equal bits of dough and roll each one into a ball. Drizzle the bites with oil, then sprinkle the remaining coconut sugar on top. Place 8 donut bites in the air fryer basket with a little space between each one. Cook for 4–5 minutes or until the center is set and the exterior just begins to brown. To prepare the rest of the donut bites, repeat the above steps.

Nutritional facts

Calories: 125, Carbohydrates: 17 g, Fat: 7 g, Protein: 1 g

2.3 English Muffin Breakfast Sandwich

Preparation Time: 15 min

Cooking Time: 5 min

Servings: 3

Ingredients

- 1 red apple
- 4 English muffins
- 3/4 cup ground cinnamon
- 1/4 cup chopped walnuts
- 1/4 cup dried cranberries

Instructions

Set the air fryer's temperature to 390°F before using. Cut the apple into quarters, remove the core, and cut into 14-inch slices lengthwise. Halve 2 English muffins and place them cut side up. Place a heaping tablespoon of cheese crumbles and a 1/4 of the apple slices on each bottom half, which will overlap slightly. Sprinkle on some cinnamon to taste. Put 1 tablespoon of nuts and 1 tablespoon of cranberries on each top half. Add a generous tablespoon of cheese on

top. Put the air fryer basket with 4 halves inside. They are not required to sit perfectly flat. You might need to allow some overlap so that all 4 can fit. Cook the muffins for 4–5 minutes until they are heated through and have a crispy bottom. Place on a platter. Seal each bun and press down firmly on top with a spatula. Repeat the steps above to construct the remaining muffins while baking the first batch. Prepare as before, then warmly serve.

Nutritional facts

Calories: 261, Carbohydrates: 12 g, Fat: 5 g, Protein: 4 g

2.4 Flourless Oat Muffins

Preparation Time: 10 min

Cooking Time: 8 min

Servings: 2

Ingredients

- 1 cup rolled oats
- 1/4 cup oat bran
- 1/4 tsp ground ginger
- 1/4 tsp salt (non-compulsory)
- 1/4 cup pecans
- 1/2 cup crushed sweet potatoes
- 3 tbsp molasses
- 8 silicone muffin cups
- Cooking spray

Instructions

Set the air fryer's temperature to 360°F. Mix the oats, oat bran, ginger, salt, and pecans in a sizable bowl. Stir in the molasses after adding the sweet potatoes. Evenly spread the sweet potatoes despite the stiffness of the mixture. To avoid sticking, lightly mist the muffin liners with cooking spray or oil. Spread the mixture evenly into the eight muffin cups; fill them well. These muffins won't rise while baking; thus, the cups will be completely full. In the air fryer basket, put 4 muffins, and cook for 6–8 minutes. Although the tops should turn dark brown, take care to prevent them from burning. To prepare the remaining muffins, repeat the steps above.

Nutritional facts

Calories: 300, Carbohydrates: 45 g, Fat: 6 g, Protein: 15 g

2.5 Lemon-Blueberry Crepes

Preparation Time: 10 min

Cooking Time: 4 min

Servings: 4

Ingredients

- 1/4 cup soft silken tofu, drained (about 2 oz)
- 1 teaspoon grated lemon zest
- 1/2 teaspoon lemon juice
- 1 1/2 teaspoons coconut sugar
- 1/2 cup fresh blueberries
- 4 (8-inch) flour tortillas

Instructions

Set the air fryer's temperature to 390°F. The tofu, sugar, lemon zest, and lemon juice should all be put in a food processor and processed until smooth. Spread each tortilla with 1 tablespoon of filling, evenly distributing it to the edges (within 12 inches). Add 2 teaspoons of blueberries on top of each tortilla, lining them up along the border. Wrap up. Put 2 tortillas in the basket of the air fryer. Crosswise, place the other 2 on top. Crepes should only be heated through and lightly browned on the outside after 4 minutes of cooking.

Nutritional facts

Calories: 123, Carbohydrates: 11 g, Fat: 1.5 g, Protein: 15 g

2.6 Oatmeal Bars

Preparation Time: 5 min

Cooking Time: 9 min

Servings: 4

Ingredients

- Oatmeal
- Oil for cooking spray
- Coconut
- Chopped pecans
- Maple syrup

Instructions

Follow the instructions on the muesli package to prepare it. Pour the muesli into a square or rectangle baking pan while it's still heated. It needs to be roughly 1/2 inch thick. Transfer a few of it into another pan if it becomes denser than that. Chill the muesli for a few hours or overnight until it is cold and hard. Cut the oats into 3- to 4-inch squares when it's time to cook. In order to create rectangles or triangles, cut each square in half. Spray the bottom of the muesli pieces with cooking spray or oil. After lightly sprinkling the tops with coconut and chopped pecans and gently pushing them in, lightly spray them with oil. Arrange the slices in a single layer, close but not touching among them, in the fryer basket. Cook at 390°F for 7–9 minutes or until the tops are browned and crispy. Put the bars on plates for serving. Sprinkle any toppings that come off after cooking over the bars and offer them warm with maple syrup.

Nutritional facts

Calories: 85, Carbohydrates: 17 g, Fat: 1 g, Protein: 2 g

2.7 Peanut Butter Breakfast Sticks

Preparation Time: 10 min

Cooking Time: 6 min

Servings: 6

Ingredients

- 2 tbsp Bob's Red Mill egg replacer
- 1/4 cup water
- 1/2 cup crushed cornflake crumbs
- Baguette loaf
- 6 tbsp almond milk
- 1 tsp pure vanilla extract
- 1/2 tsp cinnamon
- 2 tsp coconut sugar
- Cooking spray
- 1/2 cup peanut butter
- 2 large bananas, sliced

Instructions

Combine water and egg replacer in a shallow dish. Put the cornflakes' crumbs in another small bowl. Set the air fryer's temperature to 390°F. Cut the bread into "sticks" that measure about 1 x 1 x inches. Don't stress over being precise. Due to the design of the loaf, the breadstick will vary in size, but that's okay. Per serving, aim for 4 or 5 sticks. Add the almond milk, vanilla, cinnamon, and sugar to the egg mixture and well-whisked together. Dip the breadsticks in the egg, shake off the excess, then dredge them in the breadcrumbs before sprinkling them with oil or oil spray. Cook the sticks in the air fryer basket in a single layer for 3-4 minutes or until crispy and golden brown. Place on serving plates. Cook the peanut butter in the air fryer baking pan for 1 minute at 390°F; stir and continue cooking for 30 seconds more. Add sliced bananas and a generous drizzle of warm peanut butter to each serving of breakfast bars.

Nutritional facts

Calories: 109, Carbohydrates: 2 g, Fat: 8 g, Protein: 4 g

2.8 Portabella Bacon

Preparation Time: 15 min

Cooking Time: 7 min

Servings: 2

Ingredients

- 2 portabella mushrooms, stems detached
- 1 tsp smoked paprika
- 2 tsp maple syrup
- 1/8 tsp salt
- 2 tbsp oil

Instructions

With the tip of a knife, neat the portabellas closer together and remove the gills. Cut 1/4-inch-thick slices; spread them out on a cutting board. Combine the smoked paprika, maple syrup, salt, and oil in a small bowl. Spread the mushroom slices with seasoned oil on both sides. Place half of the slices in a single layer in the air fryer basket. Cook for 7 minutes at 390°F or until browned. They should not be crispy. To cook the remaining strips, repeat the above steps.

Nutritional facts

Calories: 300, Carbohydrates: 26 g, Fat: 4 g, Protein: 5 g

2.9 Strawberry Jam

Preparation Time: 10 min

Cooking Time: 15 min

Servings: 3

Ingredients

- 1 lb fresh strawberries, chopped
- 1/2 tsp grated lemon peel
- 1 tsp lemon juice
- 1 cup sugar

Instructions

Puree the strawberries in a food processor or blender. Put it in a mixing basin with the sugar, lemon juice, and peel. Fill the baking pan of the air fryer with the strawberry mixture. Cook for 5 minutes at 390°F. Cook for 5 more minutes while stirring. Cook for an additional 5 minutes after another stir. Once at room temperature, pour into a bowl.

Nutritional facts

Calories: 172, Carbohydrates: 41 g, Fat: 0.1 g, Protein: 0.3 g

2.10 Sweet Potato Toast

Preparation Time: 5 min

Cooking Time: 6 min

Servings: 1

Ingredients

- 1 sweet potato
- Oil for mist over
- Date paste
- 2 tbsp peeved coconut
- Almonds and dried cranberries for coating

Instructions

Set the air fryer's temperature to 390°F. Slice the sweet potato into rounds that are between 14 and 12 inches thick. Drizzle sweet potato slices with oil on one side. If desired, put a layer of date paste on the opposite side before turning them over. Sprinkle the coconut sparingly over the date paste and push it down to adhere. Put the potato slices in a single layer in the air fryer basket. The potato slices should only be just barely soft when cooked for 6 minutes. Top the sweet potatoes with chopped almonds and cranberries that have been dried before serving, or season them as you prefer.

Nutritional facts

Calories: 73, Carbohydrates: 17 g, Fat: 1 g, Protein: 1.3 g

2.11 Taquitos and Jam

Preparation Time: 12 min

Cooking Time: 5 min

Servings: 3

Ingredients

- 1/2 cup peanut butter
- 1/2 cup coconut chips or 1 /2 cup shredded coconut
- 2 tbsp sunflower seeds
- 8 (7-inch) corn tortillas
- Oil for cooking spray
- Strawberry Jam for dropping

Instructions

Set the air fryer's temperature to 390°F. Combine the peanut butter, coconut, and sunflower seeds in a medium bowl. Wrap the tortillas in wet paper towels and heat them in the microwave at the highest setting for 45–60 seconds or until they are warm. One at a time, prepare the tortillas, covering the others with steaming paper towels. Apply oil or frying spray to one side. Add a tablespoon of peanut butter filling to the other side of the tortilla and spread evenly to cover half. While you prepare 3 more, roll up the tortilla loosely and place it seam-side down. Place 4 tacos in a single layer in the air fryer basket. They should only brown lightly after 4–5 minutes of cooking. For the remaining taquitos, follow the steps above to stuff and fry them. Serve the taquitos hot with strawberry jam for dip because the filling will be quite hot.

Nutritional facts

Calories: 172, Carbohydrates: 41 g, Fat: 0.1 g, Protein: 0.3 g

2.12 Toast, Plain, and Simple

Preparation Time: 1 min

Cooking Time: 5 min

Servings: 1

Ingredients

- 2 slices bread

Instructions

For a better fit, cut the bread slices in half. Cook the slices for 3 minutes at 360°F in an air fryer basket. Once they have browned on both sides, turn them over and cook for another 1–2 minutes.

Nutritional facts

Calories: 150, Carbohydrates: 9 g, Fat: 12 g, Protein: 1.5 g

2.13 Veggie Sausage Corn Muffins

Preparation Time: 12 min

Cooking Time: 6 min

Servings: 3

Ingredients

- Cooking spray
- 1 cup veggie crumbles
- 1/4 tsp thyme
- 1/4 tsp cleaned sage
- 1/8 tsp allspice grounded
- 1/8 tsp ground nutmeg Corn Muffins
- 1 tbsp flaxseed meal
- 2 tbsp water
- 10 silicone muffin cups
- 3/4 cup all-purpose white flour
- 3/4 cup yellow cornmeal
- 2 1/2 tsp baking powder
- 1/4 tsp salt
- 3/4 cup almond milk
- 3 tbsp vegan butter, melted
- Strawberry Jam

Instructions

Add all of the ingredients for the vegetarian sausage to the baking pan of the air fryer, and whisk. Stirring every 2 minutes for the final 5–6 minutes of cooking at 390°F; place aside. In the meantime, combine the flaxseed meal and water in a medium bowl, and put it aside. Remove the paper liners from the aluminum foil muffin pans and save them for later use. Again, silicone is recommended. Apply a little oil or cooking spray to the muffin tins. Set the air fryer to 390°F before use. Mix the flour, cornmeal, baking soda, and salt in a large bowl. Combine the flaxseed mixture with milk and melted butter. Mix the dry ingredients thoroughly before adding the flaxseed mixture. Add the crumbled cooked vegetarian sausage. Fill the muffin cups with the prepared mixture. Insert a toothpick into the muffin tins' center; it should come out clean after 10–12 minutes of baking. Place the muffin cups in the air fryer basket. Bake the remaining muffins by repeating the above steps. Open the muffins and top them with warm strawberry jam or applesauce to serve.

Nutritional facts

Calories: 110, Carbohydrates: 4 g, Fat: 6 g, Protein: 8 g

Chapter 3:
Recipes for Lunch

3.1 Bell Peppers Stuffed with Hopping John

Preparation Time: 22 min

Cooking Time: 10 min

Servings: 3

Ingredients

- 3 bell peppers
- 1 cup cooked black-eyed peas
- 1 cup cooked brown rice
- 1/4 cup onion
- 1 tbsp Cajun seasoning mix
- 1 tbsp smoked paprika
- Salt and pepper to taste

Instructions

To form a cap, trim the bell peppers' stem ends by about 12 inches, then set them aside. Scoop out and discard the seeds and ribs. Place the peppers in a saucepan and fill it with water. Boil the water for five minutes after bringing it to a boil. Remove the peppers from the water and rinse them under cool running water. Combine the peas, rice, onion, Cajun seasoning, and smoked paprika in a small bowl. As needed, season with salt and pepper after tasting. Spoon the filling into the shells. Put the replacement pepper caps in the air fryer basket. Cook for 10 minutes at 360°F.

Nutritional facts

Calories: 500, Carbohydrates: 35 g, Fat: 31 g, Protein: 34 g

3.2 Black Bean Burgers

Preparation Time: 15 min

Cooking Time: 15 min

Servings: 3

Ingredients

- 1 can (15 oz) black beans, drained and rinsed
- 1/2 cup cooked quinoa
- 1/2 cup shredded sweet potato
- 1/4 cup chopped red onion
- 2 tsp ground cumin
- 1 tsp ground coriander seed
- 1/2 tsp salt
- Cooking spray

Instructions

Use a fork or potato blender to mash the beans in a medium basin. Stir to combine the quinoa, sweet potato, onion, cumin, coriander, and salt. Create 4 roughly 3/4-inch thick patties out of the mixture. Spray the patties with cooking spray or oil on both sides. Add the bean burgers to the air fryer basket, coat with cooking spray or oil, and fry for 15 minutes at 390°F.

Nutritional facts

Calories: 360, Carbohydrates: 44 g, Fat: 15 g, Protein: 18 g

3.3 Bread Pockets

Preparation Time: 10 min

Cooking Time: 10 min

Servings: 2

Ingredients

- 4 heavy bread slices
- Oil for mist over
- 4 heaping tbsp axed mushrooms
- 1/4 cup axed black olives
- Pizza sauce (non-compulsory)

Instructions

Apply oil to the bread slices on both sides. Place the slices upright and make a deep pocket by cutting a hole in the top of the bread. Be careful not to cut through the edges or the bottom as you cut almost to the bottom crust. Add a tablespoon of olives and chopped mushrooms to each bread pocket. Place the bread pockets in the air fryer basket standing up. Cook the filling and bread at 360°F for 8–10 minutes or until they are both heated. Serve hot, if desired, with pizza sauce or another dipping sauce.

Nutritional facts

Calories: 300, Carbohydrates: 26 g, Fat: 4 g, Protein: 5 g

3.4 Brown Rice Bake

Preparation Time: 4 min

Cooking Time: 8 min

Servings: 4

Ingredients

- 1 tsp sesame oil
- 1/3 cup chopped onion
- 1/3 cup chopped bell pepper
- 2 cups cooked brown rice
- 1 can (8 oz) crushed pineapple
- 1/2 tsp salt

Instructions

Place the oil, onion, and bell pepper in the baking pan; heat for 1 minute while stirring. Cook the combination of vegetables for 3–4 minutes more until tender. Place the rice, pineapple, and salt in a bowl with the vegetables, and toss to combine. Pour the mixture into the air fryer baking pan and heat everything through for 2–3 minutes at 390°F.

Nutritional facts

Calories: 218, Carbohydrates: 45 g, Fat: 1.6 g, Protein: 4 g

3.5 Burritos

Preparation Time: 12 min

Cooking Time: 10 min

Servings: 3

Ingredients

- 1 cup vegan refried beans
- 1 tbsp Seasoning
- 5 (10-inch) flour tortillas
- 1/2 cup sliced black olives
- 1/2 cup drained and sliced jalapeños
- 1 cup Cheddar-style shreds

Instructions

Combine the spices and beans in a small bowl. Place 1/4 cup of beans on each tortilla, about 2 inches from the edge. Add a fourth of the olives, jalapeños, and cheese on top of the beans. Fold the closest edge of the tortilla over the filling and roll it up once. Roll up completely after folding on each side. Put 2 burritos, seam side down, in the air fryer basket. Place the remaining 2 burritos on top of the first 2, cooked side down and crosswise. Cook for 5 minutes at 390°F. Flip the top and bottom layers of the burritos as you reposition them. Cook the burritos for a further 5 minutes or until they are heated through.

Nutritional facts

Calories: 280, Carbohydrates: 40 g, Fat: 9 g, Protein: 9 g

3.6 Aloo Patties

Preparation Time: 10 min

Cooking Time: 15 min

Servings: 3

Ingredients

- 1 cup pounded potato
- Salt to taste
- 1/4 tsp ginger chopped
- 1 green chili chopped
- 1 tsp lemon juice
- 1 tbsp coriander leaves
- 1/4 tsp red chili powder
- 1/4 tsp cumin powder

Instructions

Mix the ingredients thoroughly, paying attention to the flavors. Combine the ingredients to form patties, which you will roll out well. Preheat the outside of the fryer to 250°F for 5 minutes. Place the patties in the Fryer's basket after opening it. Close it slowly. Maintain the air fryer at 150°F for 10–12 minutes. Turn the patties over periodically to ensure even cooking. Warm up and serve with mint chutney.

Nutritional facts

Calories: 152, Carbohydrates: 17 g, Fat: 3 g, Protein: 4 g

3.7 Mixed Vegetable Patties

Preparation Time: 20 min

Cooking Time: 8 min

Servings: 4

Ingredients

- 1 cup grated mixed vegetables
- Salt to taste
- 1/4 tsp ginger chopped
- 1 green chili chopped
- 1 tsp lemon juice
- 1 tbsp coriander leaves
- 1/4 tsp red chili powder
- 1/4 tsp cumin powder

Instructions

Mix the ingredients thoroughly, paying attention to the flavors. The ingredients will now be formed into patties, which you will roll out well. Preheat the outside of the fryer to 250°F for 5 minutes. Place the patties in the Fryer's basket after opening it. Close it slowly. Maintain the air fryer at 150°F for 10–12 minutes. Rotate the patties over periodically to ensure even cooking. Warm up and serve with mint chutney.

Nutritional facts

Calories: 130, Carbohydrates: 15 g, Fat: 2 g, Protein: 2 g

3.8 Chickenless Parmesan

Preparation Time: 5 min

Cooking Time: 25 min

Servings: 3

Ingredients

- 4 oz angel hair pasta
- 2 breaded chicken-style patties
- 2 tsp grated Parmesan-style topping
- 1/2 cup spaghetti

Instructions

As directed on the package, prepare the angel hair pasta. Place the patties in the air fryer basket while waiting for the water to boil. For 10 minutes, cook the patties at 390°F. After flipping the patties, add 1 teaspoon of the Parmesan topping to each. Add 1 tablespoon of sauce to each burger, then simmer for another 10–15 minutes or until well cooked. After draining, combine the pasta with the remaining 1/2 cup of sauce. Place the patties on top after dividing the pasta into bowls or plates.

Nutritional facts

Calories: 60, Carbohydrates: 4 g, Fat: 3 g, Protein: 4 g

3.9 Chiles Rellenos

Preparation Time: 30 min

Cooking Time: 13 min

Servings: 4

Ingredients

- 2 *poblano* peppers
- 1 cup veggie crumbles grounded
- 1/4 cup minced onion
- 1 tsp light olive oil
- 1 cup fresh corn kernels
- 1 tbsp chili powder
- 1 tbsp cocoa powder
- 1/2 tsp salt
- 1/2 cup all-purpose flour
- 1/8 tsp salt
- 3/4 cup almond milk
- 1 1/2 cups breadcrumbs
- 1 cup all-purpose white flour
- Cooking spray
- 1/4 cup red salsa for serving

Instructions

Cut a slit through each poblano on one side by laying them out flat. Place the peppers in a small pot and fill it with water. Boil the mixture for 5 minutes. Remove the poblanos from the pan and wash them under cold running water. Prepare the filling while the poblanos are boiling. Cook the crumbs and onion in oil in a baking dish at 390°F for 3 minutes. Add salt, chili powder, cocoa powder, and corn to the mixture. Place the filling inside the peppers, and then secure them with toothpicks. Combine all of the batter's ingredients in a small bowl. Place the panko crumbs on a piece of wax paper. Put the flour onto another wax paper sheet. Spoon the flour carefully around the packed poblanos. Spoon the batter over the peppers in the bowl, covering them completely. Put the panko on all sides of the battered poblanos before dredging them. Spray the peppers with oil, placed them gently in the air fryer basket, and cook for 10 minutes at 390°F or until browned and crispy. Before serving, remove the toothpicks and add salsa to the poblanos.

Nutritional facts

Calories: 394, Carbohydrates: 24 g, Fat: 29 g, Protein: 14 g

3.10 Coconut Tofu

Preparation Time: 40 min

Cooking Time: 6 min

Servings:

Ingredients

- 14 block extra-firm tofu, pressed
- 1 1/2 cups pineapple juice
- 2 tbsp Bob's Red Mill egg replacer
- 3/4 cup shredded coconut
- 3/4 cup breadcrumbs
- Salt to taste
- Cooking spray

Instructions

Cut cubes of tofu into 12 inches in size. Cover tofu with pineapple juice and marinate for 30 minutes. Drain the tofu, and then save the marinade. Mix the egg substitute with 1/4 cup of the saved liquid in a small bowl. Allow it to thicken for a minute. Mix the breadcrumbs and coconut in another shallow bowl. Add salt to taste to the tofu. Set the air fryer to 390°F before use. To the egg wash, add 3 additional tablespoons of the pineapple juice that was set aside, and stir until combined. Dip the tofu in the egg wash and then roll it in the coconut mixture, working with a few pieces at a time. Spray the tofu cubes with oil or cooking spray before arranging them in a single layer, near to one another, but not touching, in the air fryer basket. Cook till pale golden brown for 5–6 minutes. To prepare the rest of the tofu, repeat the above steps.

Nutritional facts

Calories: 134, Carbohydrates: 6.7 g, Fat: 9 g, Protein: 18 g

3.11 Empanadas

Preparation Time: 30 min

Cooking Time: 22 min

Servings: 3

Ingredients

- 9 oz package chicken-style strips
- Oil for mist over
- 1 can (4 oz) chopped green chills
- 1/4 cup chopped tomatoes
- 1/2 tsp cumin
- 1/2 tsp thyme
- 1 cup Masa Harina flour
- 1/2 cup all-purpose white flour
- 1/2 tsp baking powder
- 1/4 tsp salt
- 1/2 cup water
- 1/4 cup almond milk

Instructions

Make the filling first. After spraying the chicken-style strips with oil, place them in the air fryer basket. Cook for 2 minutes at 360°F. Blot the chopped green chills using paper towels to remove extra moisture. Chop the chicken-style strips coarsely and combine with the cumin, thyme, tomatoes, chilies, and sun-dried chiles. Make the dough next. Mix the Masa Harina, white flour, baking soda, and salt in a medium bowl. For soft dough, combine the milk and water and stir. Roll each of the 8 sections of dough into a ball. Make a 4-inch circle out of each ball. Over the rounds of dough, distribute the filling mixture equally. Make a half-moon pie by moistening the circle edges with a finger dipped in water and folding them over. Using a fork, seal the edges. In the fryer basket, place 4 empanadas, and cook for 5 minutes at 360°F. Cook the empanadas for 5–10 minutes until light brown. The remaining empanadas can be cooked by repeating the above steps.

Nutritional facts

Calories: 183, Carbohydrates: 22 g, Fat: 5 g, Protein: 11 g

3.12 Fishless Sticks with Remoulade

Preparation Time: 5 min

Cooking Time: 5 min

Servings: 3

Ingredients

- 1 package (7 oz) frozen fishless sticks (10 counts) Remoulade
- 1/2 cup vegan mayonnaise
- 2 tbsp ketchup
- 1 tbsp yellow mustard
- 1 tbsp tarragon vinegar
- 1/4 onion, grated
- Salt to taste

Instructions

Set the air fryer to 390°F before using. Place all the fishless sticks in the fryer basket and cook for 5 minutes to heat through. Extra oil is not required for crisping. Stir the sauce ingredients while the air fryer is heating up and cooking. Serve the Remoulade beside the fishless sticks for dipping.

Nutritional facts

Calories: 280, Carbohydrates: 40 g, Fat: 9 g, Protein: 9 g

3.13 Italian Pita Pockets

Preparation Time: 10 min

Cooking Time: 13 min

Servings: 2

Ingredients

- 2 green or red bell peppers
- Oil for mist over
- 4 pita pocket splits
- 1/4 cup marinara sauce

Instructions

Cut the bell pepper into strips between 14 and 38 centimeters wide. Oil the pepper strips before placing them in the air fryer basket. Cook the peppers for 8 minutes at 390°F or until they are soft. Remove the entire contents of the basket. Place 1/4 of the bell pepper strips and 1 tablespoon of marinara sauce in each pita pocket. Put the pita halves in the air fryer basket so that they are resting against the sides of the basket and one another while standing up. To fully heat, cook for 4–5 minutes at 390°F. Serve warm.

Nutritional facts

Calories: 300, Carbohydrates: 26 g, Fat: 4 g, Protein: 5 g

3.14 Mushroom Galette

Preparation Time: 10 min

Cooking Time: 15 min

Servings: 4

Ingredients

- 2 cups shared mushrooms
- 1 1/2 cups coarsely crushed peanuts
- 3 tsp chopped ginger
- 1–2 tbsp coriander leaves
- 3 green chilies chopped
- 1 1/2 tbsp lemon juice
- 2 tbsp garam masala
- Salt and pepper to taste

Instructions

In a fresh bowl, combine the ingredients. Shape this mixture into flat, circular galettes. Moisten the galettes lightly with water. Sprinkle the crushed peanuts over each galette. Preheat the fryer for five minutes at 160°F. Cook the galettes for 25 minutes at the same temperature in the frying basket. Roll them over often to obtain a consistent cook. Serve with ketchup or mint chutney.

Nutritional facts

Calories: 240, Carbohydrates: 33 g, Fat: 17 g, Protein: 12 g

3.15 Balsamic Artichokes

Preparation Time: 10min

Cooking Time: 7 min

Servings: 4

Ingredients

- 4 large artichokes
- Salt and black pepper to taste
- 2 tbsp lemon juice
- 1/4 cup olive oil
- 2 tsp balsamic vinegar
- 1 tsp oregano, dried
- 2 garlic cloves, minced

Instructions

Season the artichokes with salt and pepper, coat them with 1/2 of the oil and 1/2 of the lemon juice, place them in the fryer, and cook them for 7 minutes at 360°F. In the meantime, thoroughly combine the remaining lemon juice, vinegar, oil, salt, pepper, garlic, and oregano in a bowl. Place the artichokes in a serving tray, top with the balsamic vinaigrette, and serve.

Nutritional facts

Calories: 200, Carbohydrates: 12 g, Fat: 3 g, Protein: 4 g

3.16 Black Gram Galette

Preparation Time: 10min

Cooking Time: 6min

Servings: 3

Ingredients

- 2 cups black gram
- 2 potatoes boiled and pounded
- 1 1/2 coarsely crushed peanuts

- 3 tsp chopped ginger
- 2 tbsp fresh coriander leaves
- 3 green chilies chopped
- 1 1/2 tbsp lemon juice
- Salt and pepper to taste

Instructions

In a fresh bowl, combine the ingredients. Shape this mixture into flat, circular galettes. Moisten the galettes lightly with water. Preheat the Air Fryer to 160°F for five minutes. Cook the galettes for 25 minutes at the same temperature in the fry basket. Roll them over often to obtain a consistent cook. Serve either with ketchup or mint chutney.

Nutritional facts

Calories: 340, Carbohydrates: 59 g, Fat: 1.5 g, Protein: 25 g

3.17 Stuffed Eggplant Baskets

Preparation Time: 10 min

Cooking Time: 6 min

Servings: 2

Ingredients

- 6 eggplants
- 1/2 tsp salt
- 1/2 tsp pepper powder

For the filling:

- 1 onion finely chopped
- 1 green chili chopped
- 1 1/2 tbsp chopped coriander leaves
- 1 tsp fenugreek
- 1 tsp dried mango powder
- 1 tsp cumin powder
- Salt and pepper to taste
- 1 tsp red chili flakes
- 1/2 tsp oregano
- 1/2 tsp basil
- 1/2 tsp parsley

Instructions

Combine all the ingredients listed under "Filling" in a bowl. Eliminate the eggplant's stem. Remove the caps. Take some of the flesh out as well. On the inside of the eggplants, season with salt and pepper. Set them aside for a while. Fill the eggplant now, leaving a tiny space at the top, with the prepared filling. Seasoning is now added. Preheat the Air Fryer to 140°F for 5 minutes. Fill the fry basket with the eggplants, then secure it. Continue cooking for another 20 minutes at the same temperature. To avoid overcooking, flip them over every few minutes.

Nutritional facts

Calories: 152, Carbohydrates: 19 g, Fat: 5 g, Protein: 5 g

3.18 Mujadarra

Preparation Time: 10 min

Cooking Time: 50 min

Servings: 4

Ingredients

- 2 sweet onions, finely sliced
- 2 tbsp olive oil
- Salt to taste
- 1 cup canned lentils
- 1 cup cooked brown rice
- 1/2 cup vegetable broth
- 1/2 tsp ground cumin
- 2 tbsp chopped fresh cilantro
- Lime slices, for serving

Instructions

Mix the salt, onion, and oil in a medium bowl. Preheat the air fryer for 3 minutes at 400°F (200°C). Place the onions in the air fryer basket and cook for 10 minutes, thoroughly tossing halfway through. Cook until 10 minutes, tossing thoroughly halfway through at 360°F (185°C) of heat. Finally, lower the heat to 300°F (150°C) and cook for 15 minutes, tossing every 5 minutes, until the onions are crispy and golden. Remove them from the basket and place them in a medium basin. After the air fryer has cooled for ten minutes, clean it with a paper towel. In a 7-inch (18 cm) circular baking pan (3 inches/7.5 cm deep), combine half the onions, the lentils, rice, broth, and cumin. Air fry at 360°F (185°C) for 15 minutes, stirring halfway through or until heated through. Serve the rice and lentils with the rest of the caramelized onions, cilantro, and lime wedges on top.

Nutritional facts

Calories: 222, Carbohydrates: 45 g, Fat: 5.8 g, Protein: 6 g

3.19 Brussels Sprouts and Tomatoes Mix

Preparation Time: 5 min

Cooking Time: 10 min

Servings: 4

Ingredients

- 1 lb Brussels sprouts, trimmed
- Salt and black pepper to taste
- 6 cherry tomatoes, shared
- ¼ cup onions cut
- 1 tbsp olive oil

Instructions

Season the Brussels sprouts with salt and pepper before placing them in the air fryer and cook for 10 minutes at 350°F. Place them in a bowl with the olive oil, salt, pepper, cherry tomatoes, and green onions. Toss thoroughly, and then serve.

Nutritional facts

Calories: 121, Carbohydrates: 11 g, Fat: 4 g, Protein: 4 g

3.20 Pumpkin Lentil Curry

Preparation Time: 20 min

Cooking Time: 30 min

Servings: 2

Ingredients

- 2 cups pumpkin cubes (1/2-inch/1 cm)
- 1/2 cup chopped onion
- 1 tbsp olive oil
- 1/2 cup low-sodium vegetable broth
- 1/2 cup coconut milk
- 1 tbsp mild or hot curry powder
- 1 tsp peeled and grated ginger
- 1/2 tsp garlic, minced
- 1 cup canned lentils, rinsed and drained
- 1 cup shredded kale

Instructions

Toss the pumpkin, onion, and oil in an adequate bowl until everything is evenly covered. Place in the air fryer basket and cook until tender, stirring once or twice, for 15–18 minutes at 375°F (190°C). Cook the broth, coconut milk, curry, ginger, and garlic for about 6 minutes over medium-high heat in a medium saucepan while the pumpkin cooks. Add the lentils, kale, and curry sauce to the pumpkin mixture before transferring it to a circular baking pan 7 inches (18 cm) in diameter and 3 inches (7.5 cm) deep. Cook for 25 minutes or until well cooked. Serve.

Nutritional facts

Calories: 232, Carbohydrates: 36.6 g, Fat: 3.5 g, Protein: 13.4 g

3.21 Brussels Sprouts

Preparation Time: 10 min

Cooking Time: 8 min

Servings: 4

Ingredients

- 1 lb Brussels sprouts, washed
- Lemon juice
- Salt and black pepper to taste
- 2 tbsp peanut oil
- 3 tbsp parmesan, grated

Instructions

Place Brussels sprouts in the air fryer for 8 minutes at 350°F. Then, place them in a bowl. Whisk in the lemon juice, salt, peanut oil and pepper before adding the mixture to the Brussels sprouts. Add the parmesan and stir until it melts before serving.

Nutritional facts

Calories: 152, Carbohydrates: 8 g, Fat: 6 g, Protein: 12 g

3.22 Spicy Cabbage

Preparation Time: 10 min

Cooking Time: 8 min

Servings: 4

Ingredients

- 1 cabbage
- 1 tbsp sesame seed oil
- 1 carrot, peeved
- 1/4 cup apple vinegar
- 1/4 cup apple juice
- 1/2 tsp cayenne pepper
- 1 tsp red pepper flakes

Instructions

Combine cabbage with oil, carrot, vinegar, apple juice, cayenne, and pepper flakes in a pan that will fit your air fryer. Toss, add the mixture to the air fryer, and cook at 350°F for 8 minutes. Distribute the cabbage mixture on the plates.

Nutritional facts

Calories: 100, Carbohydrates: 11 g, Fat: 4 g, Protein: 7 g

3.23 Sweet Baby Carrots Dish

Preparation Time: 10 min

Cooking Time: 10 min

Servings: 4

Ingredients

- 2 cups carrots
- salt and black pepper to taste
- 1 tbsp brown sugar
- 1/2 tbsp olive oil

Instructions

Combine the baby carrots with oil, salt, pepper, and sugar in a dish that will fit your air fryer. Toss, place the dish in the air fryer, and cook for 10 minutes at 350°F. Serve after dividing among plates.

Nutritional facts

Calories: 100, Carbohydrates: 7 g, Fat: 2 g, Protein: 4 g

3.24 Collard Greens Mix

Preparation Time: 10 min

Cooking Time: 10 min

Servings: 4

Ingredients

- 1 bunch collard greens
- 2 tbsp olive oil
- 2 tbsp tomato puree

- 1 onion, chopped
- 3 garlic cloves, minced
- Salt and black pepper to taste
- 1 tbsp balsamic vinegar
- 1 tsp sugar

Instructions

Combine oil, garlic, vinegar, onion, and tomato puree in a dish that will fit your air fryer and stir to combine. Add the collard greens, salt, pepper, and sugar, and cook in the air fryer for 10 minutes at 320°F. Serve the mixed collard greens in portions on plates.

Nutritional facts

Calories: 121, Carbohydrates: 7 g, Fat: 3 g, Protein: 3 g

3.25 Crispy Chinese Eggplant with Soy Honey Sauce

Preparation Time: 15 min

Cooking Time: 20 min

Servings: 2

Ingredients

- 1 eggplant, cut into 1-inch pieces
- 2 tbsp olive oil
- 1 tbsp sesame oil
- 2 scallions, white and green parts
- 2 tsp minced garlic
- 2 tsp peeled and grated fresh ginger
- 1/4 cup low-sodium soy sauce
- 2 tbsp rice wine vinegar
- 2 tbsp honey Pinch red pepper flakes
- 2 tbsp water
- 1 tsp cornstarch
- 1 tbsp sesame seeds

Instructions

Toss the eggplant with the olive oil in a medium bowl to completely coat it. Preheat the Air Fryer to 375°F (190°C) for 3 minutes. Place the eggplant in the air fryer basket and cook for 20–22 minutes, flipping halfway through, until very crispy and golden. Sauté the onions, garlic, and ginger in a large skillet with the sesame oil over medium heat for 2 minutes while the eggplant cooks. Cook for 2 minutes after adding the red pepper flakes, vinegar, honey, and soy sauce. Stir the water and cornstarch in a small bowl until a pasty consistency is achieved. Stir the mixture for 30 seconds after adding it to the skillet to thicken the sauce. Turn off the skillet heat until the eggplant is cooked through. Toss the sauce-coated crispy eggplant in the skillet after adding it. Serve the dish with a sprinkle of sesame seeds.

Nutritional facts

Calories: 152, Carbohydrates: 19 g, Fat: 5 g, Protein: 5 g

3.26 Herbed Eggplant and Zucchini Mix

Preparation Time: 10 min

Cooking Time: 8 min

Servings: 4

Ingredients

- 1 eggplant cubed
- 3 zucchinis, cubed
- 2 tbsp lemon juice
- Salt and black pepper to taste
- 1 tsp thyme
- 1 tsp oregano, dried
- 3 tbsp olive oil

Instructions

Put the eggplant in a dish that will fit in your air fryer. Add the zucchini, lemon juice, salt, pepper, thyme and oregano. Toss. Place the dish in your air fryer. Cook for 8 minutes at 360°F. Distribute among plates, then serve immediately.

Nutritional facts

Calories: 152, Carbohydrates: 19 g, Fat: 5 g, Protein: 5 g

3.27 Flavored Fennel

Preparation Time: 10 min

Cooking Time: 8 min

Servings: 4

Ingredients

- 2 fennel bulbs, 1/4s
- 3 tbsp olive oil
- Salt and black pepper to taste
- 1 garlic clove, minced
- 1 red chili pepper
- ¾ cup veggie stock
- 1/2 lemon juice
- 1/4 cup white wine
- 1/4 cup parmesan, grated

Instructions

With the oil already heated in a pan that will accommodate your air fryer, add the garlic and chili pepper, mix, and cook for 2 minutes. Combine the fennel, salt, pepper, stock, wine, lemon juice, and parmesan in your air fryer. Toss to combine. Cook for 6 minutes at 350°F. Distribute among plates, then serve immediately.

Nutritional facts

Calories: 100, Carbohydrates: 4 g, Fat: 4 g, Protein: 4 g

3.28 Okra and Corn Salad

Preparation Time: 10min

Cooking Time: 12min

Servings: 6

Ingredients

- 1 lb okra, cut
- 6 scallions, sliced
- 3 green bell peppers, sliced
- Salt and black pepper to taste
- 2 tbsp olive oil
- 1 tsp sugar
- 28 oz canned tomatoes, cut
- 1 cup corn

Instructions

Heat the oil over medium-high heat in a skillet that fits your air fryer before adding the peppers and scallions; stir and cook for 5 minutes. Add the okra, tomatoes, corn, salt, pepper, and sugar to the air fryer. Stir everything together and cook for 7 minutes at 360°F. Divide the warm okra mixture among the plates.

Nutritional facts

Calories: 152, Carbohydrates: 18 g, Fat: 4 g, Protein: 4 g

3.29 Air Fried Leeks

Preparation Time: 10 min

Cooking Time: 7 min

Servings: 4

Ingredients

- 4 leeks, neat, ends cut off and shared
- Salt and black pepper to taste
- 1 tbsp olive oil
- 1 tbsp lemon juice

Instructions

Rub the leeks with oil, salt and pepper, and cook for 7 minutes at 350°F in an air fryer. Place on a dish, top with lemon juice, and serve.

Nutritional facts

Calories: 100, Carbohydrates: 6 g, Fat: 4 g, Protein: 2 g

3.30 Crispy Potatoes and Parsley

Preparation Time: 10 min

Cooking Time: 10 min

Servings: 4

Ingredients

- 1 lb gold potatoes, cut into slices
- Salt and black pepper to taste
- 2 tbsp olive

- 1/2 lemon juice
- 1/2 cup parsley leaves, cut

Instructions

In your air fryer, place the potatoes, season with salt, pepper, lemon juice, and olive oil, and cook for 10 minutes at 350°F. Distribute among plates, cover with parsley, and serve.

Nutritional facts

Calories: 152, Carbohydrates: 17 g, Fat: 3 g, Protein: 4 g

3.31 Simple Stuffed Tomatoes

Preparation Time: 10 min

Cooking Time: 15 min

Servings: 4

Ingredients

- 4 tomatoes, pulp taken and chopped
- Salt and black pepper to taste
- 1 onion, chopped
- 1 tbsp olive oil
- 2 tbsp celery, chopped
- 1/2 cup mushrooms, chopped
- 1 tbsp bread crumbs
- 1/4 tsp caraway seeds
- 1 tbsp parsley, chopped

Instructions

Put olive oil in a pan over medium heat. Add the onion and celery, stir, and cook for 3 minutes. Add the mushrooms and tomato pulp; stir and simmer for another minute. Stir in the caraway seeds, parsley, salt, and pepper. Cook for a further 4 minutes, and then turn off the heat. Place tomatoes in your air fryer, stuff with this mixture, and cook for 8 minutes at 350°F. Serve the filled tomatoes on individual plates.

Nutritional facts

Calories: 143, Carbohydrates: 4 g, Fat: 4 g, Protein: 4 g

3.32 Indian Potatoes

Preparation Time: 10 min

Cooking Time: 12 min

Servings: 4

Ingredients

- 1 tbsp coriander seeds
- 1 tbsp cumin seeds
- Salt and black pepper to taste
- 1/2 tsp turmeric powder
- 1/2 tsp red chili powder
- 1 tsp pomegranate powder
- 1 tbsp pickled mango, chopped
- 2 tsp fenugreek, dried
- 5 potatoes, boiled and cubed
- 2 tbsp olive oil

Instructions

Add the coriander and cumin seeds to a frying pan filled with oil that fits your air fryer and heat over medium heat for 2 minutes. Add potatoes, mango, fenugreek, salt, pepper, turmeric, chili powder, pomegranate powder, and toss. Place in your air fryer and cook for 10 minutes at 360°F. Divide among plates, then warmly serve.

Nutritional facts

Calories: 251, Carbohydrates: 12 g, Fat: 7 g, Protein: 7 g

3.33 Broccoli and Tomatoes Air Fried Stew

Preparation Time: 10 min

Cooking Time: 20 min

Servings: 4

Ingredients

- 1 broccoli head
- 2 tsp coriander seeds
- 1 tbsp olive oil
- 1 onion, chopped
- Salt and black pepper to taste
- A pinch red pepper
- 1 ginger piece, sliced
- 1 garlic clove, minced
- 28 oz canned tomatoes, pureed

Instructions

Add the onions, salt, pepper and red bell pepper to an air fryer-compatible skillet previously heated with oil over medium heat. Then stir the pan and continue cooking for 7 minutes. Stir in tomatoes, broccoli, ginger, garlic, and coriander seeds, and then cook for 12 minutes at 360°F in your air fryer. After dividing, serve in bowls.

Nutritional facts

Calories: 150, Carbohydrates: 7 g, Fat: 4 g, Protein: 12 g

3.34 Curried Roasted Cauliflower Salad

Preparation Time: 15 min

Cooking Time: 15 min

Servings: 4

Ingredients

- 1 cauliflower head
- 1 russet potato, cut into 1/2-inch cubes
- 1 tbsp olive oil
- 2 tsp curry powder
- 1/2 tsp ground cumin
- 1/4 tsp ground coriander
- 1/2 tsp garlic powder
- Tweak cayenne pepper
- 1/2 cup cranberries, dried
- 1 scallion chopped
- 3 tbsp chopped fresh parsley
- 3 tbsp coconut milk
- 3 tbsp tahini
- 1/2 lemon juice
- 1 tbsp maple syrup
- 1/2 tsp peeled and grated ginger

Instructions

Toss the cauliflower, potatoes, olive oil, curry powder, cumin, coriander, garlic powder, and cayenne pepper in a large basin until everything is well coated. Preheat the air fryer for 3 minutes at 195°C (390°F). Place the vegetables in the air fryer basket and cook for 15 minutes, stirring once halfway through cooking, until tender. When the cauliflower is cooking, combine the coconut milk, tahini, ginger, lemon juice, and maple syrup. Add the cranberries, onion, and parsley to the cauliflower mixture in a big bowl. Add the dressing, then serve.

Nutritional facts

Calories: 83, Carbohydrates: 5 g, Fat: 5 g, Protein: 4 g

3.35 Sesame Mustard Greens

Preparation Time: 10 min

Cooking Time: 11 min

Servings: 4

Ingredients

- 2 garlic cloves, minced
- 1 lb mustard greens
- 1 tbsp olive oil
- 1/2 cup onion, sliced
- Salt and black pepper to taste
- 3 tbsp veggie stock
- 1/4 tsp dark sesame oil

Instructions

Heat the oil in a pan that fits your air fryer over medium heat before adding the onions, stirring, and browning them for 5 minutes. Stir in the garlic, stock, greens, salt, and pepper. Place the ingredients in the air fryer and cook for 6 minutes at 350°F. Divide among plates, drizzle with sesame oil, and serve.

Nutritional facts

Calories: 120, Carbohydrates: 3 g, Fat: 3 g, Protein: 7 g

3.36 Radish Hash

Preparation Time: 10 min

Cooking Time: 7 min

Servings: 4

Ingredients

- 1/2 tsp onion powder
- 1 lb radishes, sliced
- 1/2 tsp garlic powder
- Salt and black pepper to taste
- 2 tbsp Bob's Red Mill egg replacer
- 1/3 cup parmesan

Instructions

In a bowl, combine the radishes with egg replacer, parmesan, salt, pepper, onion, and garlic powder. Transfer the radishes to a pan that fits your air fryer and cook for 7 minutes at 350°F. Serve hash divided among plates.

Nutritional facts

Calories: 80, Carbohydrates: 5 g, Fat: 5 g, Protein: 7 g

3.37 Black Bean Jalapeño Tostadas

Preparation Time: 10 min

Cooking Time: 26 min

Servings: 2

Ingredients

- 2 flour or corn tortillas (6-inch)
- Olive oil, for scrubbing
- 1 cup canned low-sodium black beans
- 1/2 red bell pepper
- 1/2 jalapeño pepper, chopped
- 1/2 tsp ground cumin
- 1/2 cup crumbled queso fresco
- 1 tomato, diced
- 1 scallion, green part only
- 1 tbsp fresh cilantro chopped

Instructions

Preheat the Air fryer to 370°F (190°C for 3 minutes). Brush each tortilla with oil on both sides and cook in the air fryer basket for 8 minutes, turning halfway through, until crispy. Put a baking pan on top to prevent the tortilla from blowing away. Remove tortillas when they are crispy. Toss the beans, bell pepper, and jalapeño in a 7-inch (18-cm) circular baking pan and bake for 12-15 minutes. Put the cumin-seasoned beans and veggies in a food processor and pulse until a coarse purée forms. Cover each tostada with the bean mixture before top with cheese, tomato, scallion, and cilantro. Serve.

Nutritional facts

Calories: 120, Carbohydrates: 7 g, Fat: 8 g, Protein: 4 g

3.38 Swiss Chard and Sausage

Preparation Time: 10 min

Cooking Time: 20 min

Servings: 8

Ingredients

- 8 cups Swiss chard, chopped
- 1/2 cup onion, chopped
- 1 tbsp olive oil
- 1 garlic clove, minced
- Salt and black pepper to taste
- 2 tbsp Bob's Red Mill egg replacer
- A tweak nutmeg
- 1/4 cup parmesan, grated
- 1 lb sausage, chopped

Instructions

With the oil heated in a pan that fits your air fryer, add the onions, garlic, Swiss chard, salt, pepper and nutmeg. Stir for 2 minutes, and then turn off the heat. Whisk together the egg replacer and parmesan in a basin along with the Swiss chard mix. Add the mixture to your air fryer and cook for 17 minutes at 320ºF. Serve after dividing among plates.

Nutritional facts

Calories: 332, Carbohydrates: 14 g, Fat: 13 g, Protein: 23 g

3.39 Spanish Greens

Preparation Time: 10min

Cooking Time: 8 min

Servings: 4

Ingredients

- 1 apple, chopped
- 1 onion, sliced
- 3 tbsp olive oil
- 1/4 cup raisins
- 6 garlic cloves, sliced
- 1/4 cup pine nuts, toasted
- 1/4 cup balsamic vinegar
- 5 cups spinach and chard
- Salt and black pepper to taste
- A pinch nutmeg

Instructions

Heat an air fryer-compatible pan with oil over medium-high heat before adding onion, stirring, and cooking for 3 minutes. Stir in the apple, garlic, raisins, vinegar, mixed chard and spinach, nutmeg, salt and pepper. Place in the preheated air fryer and cook for 5 minutes at 350ºF. Distribute among plates, cover with pine nuts, and serve.

Nutritional facts

Calories: 120, Carbohydrates: 3 g, Fat: 1 g, Protein: 6 g

3.40 Flavored Air Fried Tomatoes

Preparation Time: 10 min

Cooking Time: 15 min

Servings: 8

Ingredients

- 1 jalapeño pepper, sliced
- 4 garlic cloves, minced
- 2 lb cherry tomatoes, shared
- Salt and black pepper to taste
- 1/4 cup olive oil
- 1/2 tsp oregano, dried
- 1/4 cup basil, chopped
- 1/2 cup parmesan, grated

Instructions

Combine the tomatoes with the garlic, jalapeño, salt, pepper, and oregano in a bowl. Drizzle the oil over the mixture and toss to combine. Place the mixture in the air fryer and cook for 15 minutes at 380ºF. Toss tomatoes with basil and parmesan in a bowl before serving.

Nutritional facts

Calories: 140, Carbohydrates: 6 g, Fat: 2 g, Protein: 8 g

Chapter 4: Recipes for Dinner

4.1 Meatless Loaf

Preparation Time: 15 min

Cooking Time: 40 min

Servings: 4

Ingredients

- 2 cups veggie ground crumbles
- 1/4 cup onion, minced
- 1/4 cup zucchini minced
- 1/4 cup sundried tomatoes minced
- 1/4 cup green bell pepper minced
- 1 tbsp vegan Worcestershire sauce
- 1 tbsp Bob's Red Mill egg replacer
- 2 tbsp water oil for misting or cooking spray
- 1/4 cup ketchup
- 1 tsp vegan Worcestershire sauce
- 1 tbsp blackstrap molasses

Instructions

Combine all of the loaf's ingredients in a medium bowl. Spray the baking pan with cooking or oil spray, then firmly pack the bread. Cook for 30 minutes at 360°F. Combine all of the topping ingredients while the loaf is baking. After adding the topping, bake the bread for an additional 10 minutes.

Nutritional facts

Calories: 121, Carbohydrates: 21 g, Fat: 4 g, Protein: 2 g

4.2 Mini Pizzas

Preparation Time: 10 min

Cooking Time: 4 min

Servings: 4

Ingredients

- 2 (7 oz) vegan Italian sausage links
- 2 English muffins
- 1/2 cup marinara sauce
- 1/4 cup sliced ripe olives
- 1/2 cup vegan mozzarella-style shreds

Instructions

Set the air fryer to 390°F before using. Cut each muffin in half. Next, cut each half lengthwise into eight pieces. Spread 2 teaspoons of marinara sauce on each half of the muffin. Place 2 vegan sausage slices on top, with some space between each. Place 1 tablespoon of olives between the sausage pieces in the middle of each muffin. Add 1 generous tablespoon of vegan cheese shredded on top of each muffin. In the air fryer basket, place 2 small pizzas. Cook for 4 minutes or until the cheese is melted and the bottoms of the muffins are browned. For cooking the remaining little pizzas, repeat the above steps.

Nutritional facts

Calories: 180, Carbohydrates: 33 g, Fat: 6 g, Protein: 9 g

4.3 Mushroom-Onion Hand Pies

Preparation Time: 15 min

Cooking Time: 20 min

Servings: 8

Ingredients

- 1 tbsp extra-light olive oil
- 1 1/2 cups chopped mushrooms
- 1/4 cup chopped onion
- 1 cup chopped kale (slightly packed)
- 1 tbsp lemon juice
- 1/4 tsp garlic powder
- Salt and pepper to taste
- 1 1/2 cups all-purpose white flour
- 1/4 tsp salt
- 1/3 cup coconut oil
- 8 tbsp cold water
- Cooking spray

Instructions

Make the filling first. Add the mushrooms and onions to the pan when the oil is 390°F, and cook for 5 minutes. Add the kale, lemon juice, garlic powder, and salt and pepper to taste after stirring. Set apart for cooling. Make the crust next. Combine the flour and salt in a large bowl. Add the coconut oil and mix with a pastry blender. Stir in 6 tablespoons of water. Add the remaining water while stirring to obtain a consistent pie crust. Cut the dough into eight pieces. Each piece of dough is patted into a circle with a diameter of about 5 inches. Evenly distribute the filling among the dough rounds. Fold each dough circle into the shape of a half-moon, and Close the sides tightly with a fork. Place all 8 pies in the air fryer basket after coating both sides of each hand pie with cooking spray or oil. Cook for 10 minutes at 390°F. Spray the pies with more oil if they aren't browning properly. Cook the pies for 5 minutes until golden, and the crust has cooked through.

Nutritional facts

Calories: 340, Carbohydrates: 33 g, Fat: 17 g, Protein: 12 g

4.4 Pecan-Crusted Eggplant

Preparation Time: 15 min

Cooking Time: 8 min

Servings: 4

Ingredients

- 2 tbsp Bob's Red Mill egg replacer
- 4 tbsp water
- 1 cup breadcrumbs
- 1/4 tsp salt
- 1/4 tsp pepper
- 1/4 tsp dry mustard
- 1/4 tsp marjoram
- 1/2 cup pecans
- 6 tbsp almond milk
- 1 eggplant
- cooking spray

Instructions

Combine the egg substitute and water in a medium basin and then set aside. Pulse the breadcrumbs, salt, pepper, mustard, and marjoram in a food processor to create finely ground crumbs. Add the pecans and process in short bursts until chopped. Take it easy to avoid overdoing it. Set the air fryer to 390°F before using. Place the coating mixture on a shallow dish after removing it from the food processor. Add the almond milk to the egg mixture; whisk to incorporate thoroughly. Slice the eggplant into 1/2-inch thick pieces, and then season with salt and pepper. After coating them entirely in the crumbs, roll the eggplant slices in the milk wash. Spray each slice with oil on both sides. Place half of the eggplant slices in the air fryer basket (see at left), and cook for 6–8 minutes or until the coating is golden and crispy. To cook the remaining slices, repeat the above steps.

Nutritional facts

Calories: 86, Carbohydrates: 11 g, Fat: 4 g, Protein: 2 g

4.5 Poblano Enchiladas

Preparation Time: 29 min

Cooking Time: 20 min

Servings: 4

Ingredients

- 1 tbsp light olive oil
- 1/2 cup cubed zucchini

- 1/4 cup cubed onion
- 1/4 cup cubed poblano pepper
- 1/4 cup pounded avocado
- 7 oz can salsa verde
- 3/4 cup firm tofu, cubed
- 8–10 corn tortillas

Instructions

Add the olive oil, zucchini, onion, and poblano pepper to the air fryer baking pan. Cook the vegetables for 5 minutes at 390°F or until they are fork-tender. Return the baking pan to the air fryer after placing the vegetables in a small bowl and setting it aside. Mix the mashed avocado with 2 tablespoons of the salsa verde in a separate small bowl. Stir together the tofu cubes and avocado mixture in the bowl of vegetables. Each tortilla should have 1 tablespoon of filling down one side before being rolled up. Place four rolled tortillas in the baking dish and top each with one spoonful of salsa verde. Spread the remaining salsa over the 4 tortillas after stacking them on top of the ones in the baking dish. Cook for 15 minutes at 360°F.

Nutritional facts

Calories: 180, Carbohydrates: 26 g, Fat: 10 g, Protein: 10 g

4.6 Polenta Half-Moons with Creole Sauce

Preparation Time: 21 min

Cooking Time: 30 min

Servings: 5

Ingredients

- 14 oz frozen bag mirepoix
- 4 oz can chopped mushrooms, drained
- 2 tbsp Cajun Seasoning Mix
- 1 tbsp water,
- 1 cup all-purpose flour
- 1/2 cup almond milk
- 2 cups panko breadcrumbs
- 18 oz roll polenta
- Cooking spray

Instructions

Stir all the sauce ingredients on a baking sheet, and bake at 360°F for 5 minutes. Cook while stirring for an additional 5 minutes, then remove from heat. Set up your breading station with flour on a sheet of wax paper, milk in a shallow basin, and breadcrumbs on another sheet of wax paper while the sauce is simmering. Slice the polenta into 12-inch thick pieces. Coat the polenta discs with flour, almond milk and breadcrumbs. Lay each slice out on a cutting board, then split each in half to form a half-moon. Spray oil or cooking spray on all sides of the half-moons before placing half of the slices in the air fryer near one another but not touching. Cook for 15 minutes at 390°F or until crisp and lightly browned. Repeat the steps once more with the rest of the half-moon slices. Pour 1 tablespoon of the Creole Sauce over every half-moon before serving.

Nutritional facts

Calories: 80, Carbohydrates: 17 g, Fat: 1 g, Protein: 2 g

4.7 Savory Corn Muffins

Preparation Time: 12 min

Cooking Time: 3 min

Servings: 10

Ingredients

- 1 tbsp flaxseed meal
- 2 tbsp water
- 10 foil muffin cups
- cooking spray
- 3/4 cup flour
- 1 cup cornmeal
- 2 tsp baking powder
- 1/2 tsp salt
- 1/4 tsp rubbed sage
- 1/4 tsp grounded marjoram
- 1/4 tsp grounded black pepper
- 1/2 tsp rubbed thyme
- 1/8 tsp ground nutmeg
- 1/4 cup pumpkin seeds

- 1/2 cup almond milk
- 2 tbsp extra light olive oil
- 3/4 cup canned pumpkin
- 1/4 cup cooked corn kernels, drained
- 1/4 cup black beans, drained

Instructions

In a medium bowl, combine water and flaxseed; set aside. Take off the paper liners from the muffin foil cups and set them aside for later. Add a little cooking spray to the aluminum foil. Heat the fryer to 390°F before use. Stir the flour, cornmeal, baking soda, salt, marjoram, pepper, thyme, and nutmeg in a sizable bowl. In the baking pan for the air fryer, put the pumpkin seeds. Cook for 2 minutes at 390°F. Stir the pan and, if necessary, continue cooking for up to another minute until gently toasted. Add the almond milk, olive oil, and pumpkin to a bowl and the prepared flaxseed water while the pumpkin seeds cook. Stir thoroughly to mix. Fill the bowl of the dry components with the liquid mixture. Add the corn, beans, and seeds. Only stir to moisten. Do not strike. There will be a lot of batter. Divide the mixture evenly among the muffin cups that have been prepared. In the air fryer basket, put 5 muffin cups. Bake at 390 °F for 12 to 13 minutes until a toothpick inserted in the center of a muffin comes out clean. Repeat the above steps to bake the remaining muffins.

Nutritional facts

Calories: 250, Carbohydrates: 23 g, Fat: 8 g, Protein: 9 g

4.8 Seitan Nuggets

Preparation Time: 15 min

Cooking Time: 9 min

Servings: 3

Ingredients

- 2 tsp Bob's Red Mill egg replacer
- 4 tbsp water
- 1/2 tsp salt
- 1/4 tsp oregano

- 1 tsp celery seed
- 1 tsp ground mustard
- 1/4 tsp paprika
- 1/2 tsp garlic powder
- 1/2 tsp dried basil, crushed
- 1/4 tsp black pepper
- 1/4 tsp ground ginger
- 3/4 cup panko breadcrumbs
- 2 tbsp potato starch
- 8 oz package seitan strips, traditional flavor
- Cooking spray

Instructions

Combine the egg substitute and water in a shallow container and then set aside. Combine all of the seasoning components in a small cup. Mix the breadcrumbs with 2 tablespoons of the seasoning mixture in another shallow dish. Put the potato starch into a lidded container or a plastic bag. Set the air fryer to 390°F before using. Spread the remaining spice mixture over the seitan strips after gently separating them. Place the seitan strips in the potato starch-filled bag or container and shake to coat. Dip the seitan strips in the egg wash and then roll in the seasoned crumbs, tackling a few pieces at a time. After covering each strip, spritz it with oil, put it in the air fryer baskets, and cook it for 5 minutes. Then, spray them with oil again after shaking the basket to disperse the nuggets. Cook the nuggets for 3–4 more minutes or until they are crispy and golden brown.

Nutritional facts

Calories: 190, Carbohydrates: 7 g, Fat: 4 g, Protein: 31 g

4.9 Sweet Potato Empanadas

Preparation Time: 22 min

Cooking Time: 8 min

Servings: 8

Ingredients

- 1/3 cup cooked pounded sweet potato

- 1/4 cup prepared quinoa
- 1 tbsp minced onions green
- 2 tbsp cut roasted peanuts
- 1/2 tsp curry powder
- 8 flour tortillas
- Oil for mist over

Instructions

Combine the potatoes, quinoa, onion, peanuts, and curry powder in a small bowl. Each tortilla should have a spoonful of filling in the center. Put some water on a finger or the back of a spoon and dab it all around the tortilla's edge. To create a half-moon shape, fold the tortilla in half. Press the edges tightly to close after evenly distributing the filling in the center. Spray each empanada with oil on both sides. Put the empanadas in the air fryer basket so they are near one another but not touching. Cook the empanadas for about 5–8 minutes at 390°F or until they are crispy and gently browned.

Nutritional facts

Calories: 370, Carbohydrates: 49 g, Fat: 16 g, Protein: 5 g

4.10 Tofu in Hoisin Sauce

Preparation Time: 20 min

Cooking Time: 38 min

Servings: 2

Ingredients

- 2 tbsp cornstarch
- 2 tbsp extra-virgin olive oil, divided

- 14 oz firm tofu, hard-pressed
- 7 oz jar hoisin sauce
- 2 tbsp orange juice
- 1 tsp Asian five-spice powder
- 1/2 onion, sliced
- 1/2 cup slivered bell pepper

Instructions

Put the corn flour in a tiny plastic bag, then reserve. Set aside 1 tablespoon of the oil in a separate little plastic bag. Cut the tofu into 1-inch chunks. After adding it, shake the corn flour bag to completely coat the tofu. After removing the cubes from the corn flour bag, place them in the oil bag, and shake. Cook the tofu in the air fryer basket for 17–20 minutes at 330°F. Prepare the vegetables and put them in the baking pan with the last tablespoon of oil while the tofu is cooking. Cook the vegetables at 390°F for 5 minutes after the tofu is done. Cook for 5 more minutes after stirring the vegetables. Combine the hoisin sauce, orange juice, and five spices powder in a small bowl. Cook the tofu and hoisin mixture for 5 minutes at 390°F after stirring it into the baking dish with the veggies. Cook for 3 minutes more after stirring gently.

Nutritional facts

Calories: 175, Carbohydrates: 3 g, Fat: 13 g, Protein: 11 g

4.11 Tofu Sticks with Sweet and Sour Sauce

Preparation Time: 45 min

Cooking Time: 7 min

Servings: 4

Ingredients

- 2 tbsp low-sodium soy sauce
- 1 tsp rice vinegar
- 2 tsp sesame oil
- 14 oz extra firm tofu, pressed
- 3/4 cup pineapple juice
- 1 tbsp vegan teriyaki sauce
- 1 tbsp coconut sugar

- 1/2 tsp crushed red pepper flakes
- 1/4 cup water, plus 1 tbsp
- 1 tbsp cornstarch
- 1/2 cup potato starch
- 1/2 cup almond milk
- 3/4 cup crushed cornflake crumbs
- Cooking spray

Instructions

Combine the soy sauce, vinegar, and oil in a shallow dish with a cover. Cut tofu into sticks that are roughly 12 x 34 x 3 inches in size. After adding the tofu sticks to the marinade, chill for 30 minutes. Make the sauce next. In a small pot, combine the pineapple juice, teriyaki sauce, sugar, red pepper flakes, and 1/4 cup water. Add the corn flour and the final tablespoon of water after boiling the sauce. Just until the sauce thickens, remove from the heat. Set the air fryer to 390°F when you're ready to start cooking the tofu. Put the milk in one shallow dish, the cornflake crumbs in another shallow dish, and the potato starch in a third shallow dish. Tofu sticks that have been marinated are dipped in flour, milk, and finally crumb. Place half of the tofu sticks in the air fryer basket in a single layer with space between them after being misted with oil or cooking spray. Cook them till crispy for 6–7 minutes. The crust shouldn't be scorched, but it should appear dark brown. To cook the remaining tofu sticks, repeat the above steps. Serve for dipping with the sweet and sour sauce.

Nutritional facts

Calories: 134, Carbohydrates: 6.7 g, Fat: 9 g, Protein: 18 g

4.12 Vegetable Turnovers

Preparation Time: 15 min

Cooking Time: 15 min

Servings: 8

Ingredients

- 12 oz package frozen blend vegetables, thawed
- 2 tbsp mirepoix
- 3 oz water, plus
- 1 tbsp for slurry
- 1 tbsp cornstarch
- 1 cup self-rising flour
- 2 tbsp all-vegetable shortening
- 1/2 cup almond milk
- 1/2 cup all-purpose flour for dusting
- Oil for mist over

Instructions

Make the filling first. Chop the veggies for California blend coarsely. Cook the veggies and mirepoix in 3 ounces of water in a small saucepan until the vegetables are fork-tender. Make a slurry by mixing the corn flour with 1 tablespoon of water in a small bowl. Stir the vegetable mixture into the slurry before bringing to a boil and simmer for 2–3 minutes to thicken the sauce. Remove the vegetable filling from the heat and set aside. Make the crust next. Cut the shortening into the flour in a medium bowl until it is evenly spread. Shape the dough into a smooth ball after adding the milk. Use two teaspoons of all-purpose flour to dust a clean work surface lightly. Create two equal amounts of dough. Roll out each dough ball individually to a thickness of 1/8 inch, making sure to keep each one as square as possible. Cut out four equal squares of dough. Place one tablespoon of the filling into each dough square, slightly off-center. Moisten the edges of each square with a finger that has been dipped in water. To create a triangle by folding one corner over to meet the other, push the sides together to make a turnover. To ensure a tight closure, crimp all of the edges with a fork. Spray turnovers with oil on both sides and cook for 15 minutes at 360°F. To prepare the remaining batch, repeat the above steps.

Nutritional facts

Calories: 86, Carbohydrates: 11 g, Fat: 4 g, Protein: 2 g

4.13 Italian Eggplant Stew

Preparation Time: 10 min

Cooking Time: 15 min

Servings: 4

Ingredients

- 1 onion, chopped
- 2 cloves garlic, sliced
- 1 cluster parsley, axed
- Salt and black pepper to taste
- 1 tsp oregano, dried
- 2 eggplants, cut into chunks
- 2 tbsp olive oil
- 2 tbsp capers, sliced
- 1 handful green olives
- 5 tomatoes, sliced
- 3 tbsp herb vinegar

Instructions

With the oil heated in a pan that fits your air fryer, add the eggplant, oregano, salt, and pepper. Stir and cook for 5 minutes. Before adding them to your air fryer, stir in the garlic, onion, parsley, capers, olives, vinegar, and tomatoes. Cook for 15 minutes at 360°F. After dividing, serve in bowls.

Nutritional facts

Calories: 170, Carbohydrates: 5 g, Fat: 13 g, Protein: 7 g

4.14 Rutabaga and Cherry Tomatoes Mix

Preparation Time: 10 min

Cooking Time: 15 min

Servings: 4

Ingredients

- 1 tbsp shallot, chopped
- 1 minced garlic clove
- ¾ cup cashews, soaked for 2 hours
- 2 tbsp nutritional yeast
- 1/2 cup veggie stock
- Salt and black pepper to taste
- 2 tsp lemon juice

- 1 cup tomatoes, shared
- 5 tsp olive oil
- ¼ tsp garlic powder
- 2 rutabagas, cut into thick noodles

Instructions

Add tomatoes and rutabaga noodles in a pan that will accommodate your air fryer. Drizzle the oil over them. Season with salt, black pepper, and garlic powder. Toss to combine. Cook for 15 minutes at 350°F. In the meantime, combine the garlic, shallots, cashews, vegetable stock, nutritional yeast, lemon juice, a dash of sea salt, and black pepper to taste in a food processor and pulse until well combined. Divide the pasta made from rutabaga among plates, top with tomatoes, and then serve with a sauce.

Nutritional facts

Calories: 160, Carbohydrates: 10 g, Fat: 2 g, Protein: 8 g

4.15 Garlic Tomatoes

Preparation Time: 10 min

Cooking Time: 15 min

Servings: 4

Ingredients

- 4 cloves garlic rumpled
- 1 lb mixed cherry tomatoes
- 3 thyme springs, sliced
- Salt and black pepper to taste
- 1/4 cup olive oil

Instructions

To prepare, combine tomatoes, salt, black pepper, garlic, olive oil, and thyme in a bowl. Place tomatoes in your air fryer and cook for 15 minutes at 360°F. To serve, divide the tomato mixture among dishes.

Nutritional facts

Calories: 100, Carbohydrates: 1 g, Fat: 0 g, Protein: 6 g

4.16 Vegetable Dumpling

Preparation Time: 10 min

Cooking Time: 14 min

Servings: 4

Ingredients

- 1 1/2 cups all-purpose flour
- Salt to taste
- 5 tbsp water
- 2 cups grated carrots
- 2 cups grated cabbage
- 2 tbsp olive oil
- 2 tsp ginger-garlic paste
- 2 tsp soya sauce
- 2 tsp vinegar

Instructions

Knead the dough before wrapping it in plastic wrap and set aside. Cook the filling ingredients next, ensuring the sauce is thoroughly drenched over the vegetables. After centering the filling, roll the dough. Wrap the dough around the filling, pinching the edges to seal the seam. Preheat the Air for 5 minutes at 200°F. Fill the fry basket with the dumplings, then secure it. They should continue to cook for another 20 minutes at the same temperature. It is suggested as a condiment Kewpie sauce or chili sauce.

Nutritional facts

Calories: 145, Carbohydrates: 24 g, Fat: 4 g, Protein: 4 g

4.17 Zucchini Noodles Delight

Preparation Time: 10 min

Cooking Time: 20 min

Servings: 6

Ingredients

- 2 tbsp olive oil
- 3 zucchinis
- 16 oz mushrooms, cut
- 1/4 cup sun-dried tomatoes, sliced
- 1 tsp minced garlic
- 1/2 cup cherry tomatoes, shared
- 2 cups tomatoes sauce
- 2 cups spinach, torn
- Salt and black pepper to taste
- A handful basil, sliced

Instructions

Place the zucchini noodles with salt and black pepper in a bowl and set aside for 10 minutes. Heat the oil in a pan that fits your air fryer over medium-high heat. Add garlic, stir, and cook for 1 minute. Add the mushrooms, sun-dried tomatoes, cherry tomatoes, spinach, cayenne sauce, and zucchini noodles. Stir everything together and cook for 10 minutes at 320°F in your air fryer. Sprinkle basil on top after being divided among dishes.

Nutritional facts

Calories: 120, Carbohydrates: 2 g, Fat: 1 g, Protein: 9 g

4.18 Simple Tomatoes and Bell Pepper Sauce

Preparation Time: 10 min

Cooking Time: 15 min

Servings: 4

Ingredients

- 2 red bell peppers, sliced
- 2 minced garlic cloves
- 1 lb cherry tomatoes, shared
- 1 tsp rosemary, dried

- 3 bay leaves
- 2 tbsp olive oil
- 1 tbsp balsamic vinegar
- Salt and black pepper to taste

Instructions

Combine the garlic, salt, black pepper, rosemary, bay leaves, half the oil, and half the vinegar with the tomatoes in a bowl. The tomatoes are then added to the air fryer and roasted for 15 minutes at 320°F. Blend well the bell peppers in your food processor while you add a bit of sea salt, some black pepper, the remaining oil, and the remaining vinegar. Distribute the roasted tomatoes among plates, top with the bell pepper sauce, and serve.

Nutritional facts

Calories: 123, Carbohydrates: 8 g, Fat: 1 g, Protein: 10 g

4.19 Cherry Tomatoes Skewers

Preparation Time: 30 min

Cooking Time: 6 min

Servings: 4

Ingredients

- 3 tbsp balsamic vinegar
- 24 cherry tomatoes
- 2 tbsp olive oil
- 3 minced garlic cloves
- 1 tbsp thyme, sliced
- Salt and black pepper to taste
- 2 tbsp balsamic vinegar
- 4 tbsp of olive oil

Instructions

Blend the following ingredients in a bowl: 2 tablespoons oil, 3 tablespoons vinegar, 3 garlic cloves, thyme, salt, and black pepper. Add the tomatoes, coat, and set aside for 30 minutes. Place 6 tomatoes on a skewer, then repeat with the remaining tomatoes. Introduce them to your air fryer and cook for 6 minutes at 360°F.

Combine salt, pepper, and 4 tablespoons of oil in another basin with 2 tablespoons of vinegar. Place tomato skewers on plates, then sprinkle the dressing over them to serve.

Nutritional facts

Calories: 140, Carbohydrates:2 g, Fat: 1 g, Protein: 7 g

4.20 Delicious Portobello Mushrooms

Preparation Time: 10 min

Cooking Time: 12 min

Servings: 4

Ingredients

- 10 basil leaves
- 1 cup spinach
- 3 cloves garlic, chopped
- 1 cup almonds, chopped
- 1 tbsp parsley
- 1/4 cup olive oil
- 8 cherry tomatoes, shared
- Salt and black pepper to taste
- 4 Portobello mushrooms, stems detached and sliced

Instructions

Combine basil, spinach, garlic, almonds, parsley, oil, salt, black pepper to taste, and mushroom stems in a food processor and blend thoroughly. Fill each mushroom with this mixture, then air-fried them for 12 minutes at 350°F. Serve by dividing mushrooms among plates.

Nutritional facts

Calories: 145, Carbohydrates: 6 g, Fat: 3 g, Protein: 17 g

4.21 Stuffed *Poblano* Peppers

Preparation Time: 10 min

Cooking Time: 15 min

Servings: 4

Ingredients

- 2 tsp garlic, minced
- 1 onion, chopped
- 10 *poblano* peppers, deseeded
- 1 tbsp olive oil
- 8 oz mushrooms, sliced
- Salt and black pepper to taste
- 1/2 cup cilantro, chopped

Instructions

Over medium-high heat, add the oil to a skillet. Stir in the onion and mushrooms. Cook for 5 minutes. Add the salt, pepper, cilantro, and garlic, and stir for 2 minutes. Divide this mixture into *poblanos*, place in your air fryer, and cook for 15 minutes at 350°F. Serve after dividing among plates.

Nutritional facts

Calories: 150, Carbohydrates: 7 g, Fat: 3 g, Protein: 10 g

4.22 Stuffed Baby Peppers

Preparation Time: 10 min

Cooking Time: 6 min

Servings: 4

Ingredients

- 12 baby bell peppers, cut into splits lengthwise
- ¼ tsp red pepper flakes, crushed
- 1 lb shrimp, cooked and peeled
- 6 tbsp jarred basil pesto
- Salt and black pepper to taste
- 1 tbsp lemon juice
- 1 tbsp olive oil
- A handful parsley, chopped

Instructions

Fill the bell pepper halves with the mixture of shrimp, pepper flakes, pesto, salt, black pepper, lemon juice, oil, and parsley after thoroughly mixing it in a basin. After 6 minutes of cooking at 320°F in your air fryer, arrange the peppers on trays and dish.

Nutritional facts

Calories: 130, Carbohydrates: 3 g, Fat: 2 g, Protein: 15 g

4.23 Eggplant and Garlic Sauce

Preparation Time: 10 min

Cooking Time: 10 min

Servings: 4

Ingredients

- 2 tbsp olive oil
- 2 garlic cloves, minced
- 3 eggplants, shared
- 1 red chili pepper, sliced
- 1 onion stalk, sliced
- 1 tbsp ginger, grated
- 1 tbsp soy sauce
- 1 tbsp balsamic vinegar

Instructions

Add the eggplant slices to a skillet filled with oil that fits your air fryer and heat over medium-high heat for 2 minutes. Add the following ingredients to your air fryer: chili pepper, garlic, green onions, ginger, soy sauce, and vinegar. Cook for 7 minutes at 320°F. Serve after dividing among plates.

Nutritional facts

Calories: 130, Carbohydrates: 7 g, Fat: 2 g, Protein: 9 g

4.24 Eggplant Hash

Preparation Time: 20 min

Cooking Time: 10 min

Servings: 4

Ingredients

- 1 eggplant, chopped
- 1/2 cup olive oil
- 1/2 lb cherry tomatoes, halved
- 1 tsp Tabasco sauce
- ¼ cup basil, chopped
- ¼ cup mint, chopped
- Salt and black pepper to taste

Instructions

Heat half of the oil in a pan that fits your air fryer over medium-high heat. Add the eggplant pieces, cook for 3 minutes, flip them over, cook for an additional 3 minutes, and then remove them to a bowl. Add the tomatoes to the same pan with the remaining oil and heat over medium-high heat for 1–2 minutes. Return the eggplant pieces to the pan, season with salt, black pepper, basil, mint, and Tabasco sauce, and then cook for 6 minutes at 320°F in your air fryer. Serve after dividing among plates.

Nutritional facts

Calories: 120, Carbohydrates: 8 g, Fat: 1 g, Protein: 15 g

4.25 Sweet Potatoes Mix

Preparation Time: 10 min

Cooking Time: 15 min

Servings: 4

Ingredients

- 3 sweet potatoes, diced
- 4 tbsp olive oil
- 3 minced garlic cloves
- 1 lemon juice
- Salt and black pepper to taste
- 2 tbsp balsamic vinegar
- Dill, chopped
- 2 onions, chopped
- A tweak cinnamon powder
- A tweak red pepper flakes

Instructions

Place the sweet potatoes in the basket of your air fryer. Add the garlic and half of the oil, stir well, and bake for 15 minutes at 350°F. In the meantime, mix the vinegar, lime juice, olive oil, green onions, pepper flakes, dill, salt, and pepper in a basin. Place the salad dressing in a bowl with sweet potatoes, mix to combine, and serve immediately.

Nutritional facts

Calories: 170, Carbohydrates: 5 g, Fat: 3 g, Protein: 12 g

4.26 Greek Potato Mix

Preparation Time: 10 min

Cooking Time: 20 min

Servings: 2

Ingredients

- 2 potatoes, cut into slices
- 1 onion, sliced
- 2 tbsp olive oil
- 1 carrot, chopped
- 1 tbsp flour
- 2 tbsp coconut yogurt
- Salt and black pepper as required

Instructions

Cook onions and carrots for 3-4 minutes in a skillet large enough to fit your air fryer. Combine the potatoes, flour, olive oil, salt, pepper, and bay leaf in your air fryer. Stir. Cook for 16 minutes at 320°F. Add the coconut yogurt, combine, and serve on plates.

Nutritional facts

Calories: 198, Carbohydrates: 6 g, Fat: 3 g, Protein: 8 g

4.27 Broccoli Hash

Preparation Time: 30 min

Cooking Time: 8 min

Servings: 2

Ingredients

- 10 oz mushrooms, halved
- 1 broccoli head, florets separated
- 1 minced garlic clove
- 1 tbsp balsamic vinegar
- 1 onion, chopped
- 1 tbsp olive oil
- Salt and black pepper to taste
- 1 tsp basil, dried
- 1 avocado
- A tweak red pepper flakes

Instructions

Combine the mushrooms, broccoli, onion, garlic, and avocado in a bowl. Combine vinegar, oil, salt, pepper, and basil thoroughly in a separate bowl. Pour this over the vegetables, mix to coat, and set aside for 30 minutes. Then, transfer to the basket of your air fryer and cook for 8 minutes at 350°F. Divide among the plates and serve with pepper flakes on top.

Nutritional facts

Calories: 182, Carbohydrates: 5 g, Fat: 3 g, Protein: 8 g

4.28 Air Fried Asparagus

Preparation Time: 10 min

Cooking Time: 15 min

Servings: 4

Ingredients

- 2 lb fresh asparagus, trimmed
- 1/4 cup olive oil
- Salt and black pepper to taste
- 1 tsp lemon zest
- 4 minced garlic cloves
- 1/2 tsp oregano, dried
- ¼ tsp red pepper flakes
- 2 tbsp parsley, finely chopped
- 1 lemon juice

Instructions

Combine oil, lemon zest, garlic, red pepper flakes, and oregano in a basin with a whisk. Toss in the asparagus, salt, and pepper before adding to the air fryer basket and cooking for 8 minutes at 350°F. Divide the asparagus among plates, then topped with parsley and lemon juice before serving.

Nutritional facts

Calories: 162, Carbohydrates: 12 g, Fat: 13 g, Protein: 8 g

4.29 Stuffed Eggplants

Preparation Time: 10 min

Cooking Time: 30 min

Servings: 4

Ingredients

- 4 eggplants, halved lengthwise
- Salt and black pepper to taste
- 10 tbsp olive oil
- 2 lb tomatoes, cut into shares and peeved
- 1 green bell pepper, sliced
- 1 onion, sliced
- 1 tbsp garlic, minced
- 1/2 cup cauliflower, sliced
- 1 tsp oregano, sliced
- 1/2 cup parsley, chopped
- 3 oz vegan cheese (any brand), crumbled

Instructions

Season the eggplants with salt, pepper, and 4 teaspoons of oil. After tossing, place them in your air fryer and cook for 16 minutes at 350°F. In the meantime, heat 3 tablespoons of oil in a pan over medium-high heat. Add the onion, stir, and cook for 5 minutes. Add the cauliflower, bell pepper, and garlic, stir, and simmer for 5 minutes. Remove from heat, and then whisk in the parsley, tomato, salt, pepper, oregano, and vegan cheese. Add the remaining oil to the air fryer, add the stuffed eggplants, and cook for an additional 6 minutes at 350°F. Distribute among plates, then serve immediately.

Nutritional facts

Calories: 240, Carbohydrates: 19 g, Fat: 4 g, Protein: 2 g

4.30 Green Beans and Parmesan

Preparation Time: 10 min

Cooking Time: 8 min

Servings: 4

Ingredients

- 12 oz green beans
- 2 tsp garlic, minced
- 2 tbsp olive oil
- Salt and black pepper to taste
- 2 tbsp Bob's Red Mill egg replacer
- 1/3 cup parmesan, grated

Instructions

Mix the oil, salt, pepper, garlic, and egg replacer thoroughly in a basin. Add the green beans, combine well, and top with parmesan. Add the green beans to your air fryer and cook for 8 minutes at 390°F. Serve the green beans immediately after dividing them among plates.

Nutritional facts

Calories: 120, Carbohydrates: 7 g, Fat: 8 g, Protein: 4 g

4.31 Potato Flat Cakes

Preparation Time: 10 min

Cooking Time: 15 min

Servings: 2

Ingredients

- 2 tbsp garam masala
- 2 cups sliced potato
- 3 tsp ginger finely chopped

- 2 tbsp fresh coriander leaves
- 3 green chilies chopped
- 1 1/2 tbsp of lemon juice
- Salt and pepper to taste

Instructions

Add water to the mixture of ingredients in a clean bowl. Apply the paste to the potato slices without making them too watery. For five minutes, pre-heat the air fryer to 160°F. Cook the galettes for twenty-five minutes at the same temperature after being placed in the fry basket. To obtain a uniform cook, keep rolling them over. Serve with ketchup or mint chutney, as desired.

Nutritional facts

Calories: 192, Carbohydrates: 30 g, Fat: 4 g, Protein: 3 g

4.32 Green Beans and Tomatoes

Preparation Time: 10 min

Cooking Time: 15 min

Servings: 4

Ingredients

- 1 nip cherry tomatoes
- 1 lb green beans
- 2 tbsp olive oil
- Salt and black pepper to taste

Instructions

Combine cherry tomatoes, green beans, olive oil, salt, and pepper in a bowl. Transfer the mixture to an air fryer and cook for 15 minutes at 400°F. Distribute among plates, then serve immediately.

Nutritional facts

Calories: 162, Carbohydrates: 8 g, Fat: 6 g, Protein: 9 g

4.33 Easy Green Beans and Potatoes

Preparation Time: 10 min

Cooking Time: 15 min

Servings: 5

Ingredients

- 2 lb green beans
- 6 potatoes, shared
- Salt and black pepper to taste
- A sprinkle olive oil

Instructions

In a bowl, toss green beans and potatoes with oil, salt, and pepper. Then move to your air fryer and cook for 15 minutes at 390°F. Separate among plates.

Nutritional facts

Calories: 374, Carbohydrates: 28 g, Fat: 15 g, Protein: 12 g

4.34 Flavored Green Beans

Preparation Time: 10 min

Cooking Time: 15 min

Servings: 4

Ingredients

- 1 lb red potatoes, cut into wedges
- 1 lb green beans
- 2 minced garlic cloves
- 2 tbsp olive oil
- Salt and black pepper to taste
- 1/2 teaspoon oregano, dried

Instructions

Combine potatoes, green beans, garlic, oil, salt, pepper, and oregano in a pan that will fit your air fryer. Toss, add the mixture to the air fryer, and cook for 15 minutes at 380°F. Serve after dividing among plates.

Nutritional facts

Calories: 211, Carbohydrates: 8 g, Fat: 6 g, Protein: 5 g

4.35 Potatoes and Tomatoes Mix

Preparation Time: 10 min

Cooking Time: 16 min

Servings: 4

Ingredients

- 1 lb red potatoes, divided
- 2 tbsp olive oil
- 1 cocktail cherry tomatoes
- 1 tsp sweet paprika
- 1 tbsp rosemary, chopped
- Salt and black pepper to taste
- 3 minced garlic cloves

Instructions

Toss the potatoes with the tomatoes, oil, paprika, rosemary, garlic, salt, and pepper in a bowl. Then add the mixture to your air fryer and cook for 16 minutes at 380°F. Serve after dividing among plates.

Nutritional facts

Calories: 192, Carbohydrates: 30 g, Fat: 4 g, Protein: 3 g

4.36 Balsamic Potatoes

Preparation Time: 10 min

Cooking Time: 20 min

Servings: 4

Ingredients

- 1 lb baby potatoes, halved
- 2 garlic cloves, sliced
- 2 onions, sliced
- 9 oz cherry tomatoes
- 3 tbsp olive oil
- 1 tbsp balsamic vinegar
- 2 thyme springs, sliced
- Salt and black pepper to taste

Instructions

Combine garlic, onions, oil, vinegar, thyme, salt, and pepper in your food processor. Toss the potatoes, tomatoes, and balsamic marinade together in a bowl. Place the mixture in your air fryer and cook for 20 minutes at 380°F. Serve after dividing among plates.

Nutritional facts

Calories: 301, Carbohydrates: 18 g, Fat: 6 g, Protein: 6 g

4.37 Potatoes and Special Tomato Sauce

Preparation Time: 10 min

Cooking Time: 16 min

Servings: 4

Ingredients

- 2 lbs potatoes, cubed
- 4 minced garlic cloves
- 1 onion, chopped
- 1 cup tomato sauce
- 2 tbsp basil, chopped
- 2 tbsp olive oil
- 1/2 tsp oregano, dried
- 1/2 tsp parsley, dried

Instructions

In an air fryer-compatible frying pan, heat oil over medium heat before adding the onion, stir, and cook for one to 2 minutes. Combine garlic, potatoes, parsley, tomato sauce, and oregano in your air fryer. Stir. Cook for 16 minutes at 370°F. Toss in the basil, divide the mixture among dishes, and serve.

Nutritional facts

Calories: 211, Carbohydrates: 14 g, Fat: 6 g, Protein: 6 g

4.38 Cauliflower Momos

Preparation Time: 10 min

Cooking Time: 16 min

Servings: 4

Ingredients

- 1 cup all-purpose flour

- 1/2 tsp salt
- 4 tbsp water
- 2 cups vexed cauliflower
- 2 tbsp oil
- 2 tsp ginger-garlic adhesive
- 2 tsp soya sauce
- 2 tsp vinegar

Instructions

Knead the dough before wrapping it in plastic wrap and set aside. Cook the filling ingredients, and ensure the sauce is well-drenched over the cauliflower. The dough is rolled, then squared off. In the center, place the filling. Pinch the edges of the dough together as you wrap it around the filling. Preheat the Air Fryer to 200° F for 5 minutes. Close the fry basket after adding the gnocchi. Continue cooking for another 20 minutes at the same temperature. Kewpie sauce or chili sauce is suggested as condiments.

Nutritional facts

Calories: 182, Carbohydrates: 5 g, Fat: 3 g, Protein: 8 g

4.39 Broccoli Momos

Preparation Time: 10 min

Cooking Time: 10 min

Servings: 3

Ingredients

- 1 cup all-purpose flour
- 1/2 tsp salt
- 5 tbsp water
- 2 cups grated broccoli
- 2 tbsp oil
- 2 tsp ginger-garlic paste
- 2 tsp soya sauce
- 2 tsp vinegar

Instructions

Knead the dough before wrapping it in plastic wrap and set aside. After that, prepare the filling ingredients and thoroughly coat the broccoli with sauce. The dough is rolled, then squared off. Place the filling in the center.

Pinch the edges of the dough together as you wrap it around the filling. Preheat the Air Fryer to 200°F for 5 minutes. Close the fry basket after adding the gnocchi. Continue cooking for another 20 minutes at the same temperature. Kewpie or chili sauce are suggested condiments.

Nutritional facts

Calories: 140, Carbohydrates: 2 g, Fat: 1 g, Protein: 10 g

Chapter 5: Appetizers and Snacks

5.1 Artichoke Balls

Preparation Time: 26 min

Cooking Time: 10 min

Servings: 15 balls

Ingredients

- 14 oz can artichoke hearts, drained
- 1 cup breadcrumbs
- 1 tbsp extra-virgin olive oil
- 1 tsp vegan sauce
- 1 cup nut milk
- 1 tbsp sliced onions

Instructions

To create a stiff mixture, crush all the ingredients with your hands. Form a homogeneous ball with each tablespoonful. Put the artichoke balls close together in the air fryer but not touching. Cook for 10 minutes at 390°F. At room temperature or heated, serve.

Nutritional facts

Calories: 120, Carbohydrates: 9 g, Fat: 6 g, Protein: 4 g

5.2 Asparagus Fries

Preparation Time: 15 min

Cooking Time: 7 min

Servings: 4

Ingredients

- 2 tbsp Bob's Red Mill egg replacer
- 4 tbsp water
- 3/4 cup breadcrumbs
- 1/4 cup grated Parmesan-style coating
- 1/4 tsp salt
- 1 tsp lemon pepper seasoning
- 12 oz fresh asparagus spears
- 3 tbsp almond milk
- Cooking spray

Instructions

Set the air fryer to 390°F before using. Combine the water and egg replacement in a small bowl. Put it off till it thickens. Put the breadcrumbs, Parmesan topping, salt, and lemon pepper in a container or bag that can be sealed with plastic and has a cover; shake well to combine. Snap the asparagus stalks in half if their length exceeds the breadth of your air fryer basket. Put the spears in a different lidded plastic bag or container that can be sealed. Whisk the milk into the egg mixture after adding it. Over the asparagus, pour the milk mixture. Shake to coat and then close the bag or lid completely. Let the excess egg wash run off before removing the spears. Put the spears in the bag or container with the panko mixture when they are equally coated. Arrange the asparagus stalks in the air fryer basket in a single layer, with a little space between each one. Spray some oil or cooking spray on the spears. Crosswise stack more layers on top, then mist. Continue until you've used no more than 4 or 5 layers or around half the asparagus. Cook for 5–7 minutes or until crispy and golden brown. Shake and re-mist as necessary to cover any areas that aren't browning during cooking. Cook the remaining spears by repeating the above steps.

Nutritional facts

Calories: 45, Carbohydrates: 5 g, Fat: 2.5 g, Protein: 3 g

5.3 Avocado Fries

Preparation Time: 5 min

Cooking Time: 10 min

Servings: 4

Ingredients

- 1/4 cup almond milk
- 1 tbsp lime juice
- 1/8 tsp Tabasco sauce
- 3/4 cup breadcrumbs
- 1/4 cup cornmeal
- 1/4 tsp salt
- 2 tbsp flour
- Cooking spray

Instructions

Mix the milk, lime juice, and Tabasco sauce in a small bowl. Combine the panko, cornmeal, and salt in a shallow dish. Put the flour in another small bowl. Remove the pit from the avocado before cutting it in half. Lift the avocado halves from the skin with a spoon. Slice each half of an avocado crosswise into 1/2-inch thick pieces. Dip the slices in flour, then milk mixture, and finally, breadcrumbs. Mist with cooking spray or oil. Cook the coating for 10 minutes at 390°F or until it turns crispy and brown. Serve hot

Nutritional facts

Calories: 437, Carbohydrates: 28 g, Fat: 33 g, Protein: 10 g

5.4 Avocado Taquitos

Preparation Time: 15 min

Cooking Time: 8 min

Servings: 4

Ingredients

- 1 avocado
- 12 corn tortillas
- Cooking spray
- Chili powder for covering

For the filling:

- 1/2 cup refried pinto beans
- 1/4 cup corn kernels
- 2 tbsp chopped onion
- 1/2 tsp lime juice
- 1/2 tsp garlic powder
- 1/2 tsp chili powder
- 1/2 tsp cumin

Instructions

Combine all filling ingredients and set aside. Remove the avocado's pit before halving it. Lift the avocado halves from the skin with a spoon. Cut 12 thin slices of avocado lengthwise. Wrapping the tortillas in damp paper towels and heating them in the microwave for 30–60 seconds on high can help make rolling the tortillas simpler. Put 1 tablespoon of filling on each tortilla one at a time. Add a slice of avocado on top, then roll up. With toothpicks, secure. Sprinkle chili powder on top after applying oil or cooking spray to the taquito. Put 6 tacos in the air fryer basket, 3 stacked crosswise on top of the other 3. Cook for 6–8 minutes at 390°F or until they are crispy and browned. To cook the remaining taquitos, repeat the above steps. Serve.

Nutritional facts

Calories: 250, Carbohydrates: 35 g, Fat: 10 g, Protein: 8 g

5.5 Banana Fries

Preparation Time: 10 min

Cooking Time: 5 min

Servings: 6

Ingredients

- 1/2 cup crushed cornflakes
- 1/2 cup finely chopped peanuts
- 1/4 cup potato starch
- 1/4 cup maple syrup
- 2 bananas
- Cooking spray

Instructions

Set the air fryer to 390°F before using. Combine the peanuts and cornflake crumbs in a small bowl. Put the potato starch in another shallow dish. Pour the syrup into a third shallow dish. Cut the bananas in half crosswise. Cut each half lengthwise into four equal pieces to create 16 "sticks." Dip the banana sticks in potato starch and then tap to remove excess. Dip the bananas in the syrup after coating them in the crumb mixture and oil or cooking spray. Put a single layer of banana sticks in the air fryer basket. If necessary, you can stack some of them crosswise, just make sure the basket isn't too full, or they won't brown well. Cook for 4–5 minutes or until crispy and golden brown. Repeat the above steps to boil the rest of the bananas.

Nutritional facts

Calories: 45, Carbohydrates: 5 g, Fat: 2.5 g, Protein: 3 g

5.6 Battered Cauliflower

Preparation Time: 27 min

Cooking Time: 15 min

Servings: 4

Ingredients

- 1 cup all-purpose flour
- 1 tbsp ground flaxseed
- 1 cup almond milk

- 2 cups panko breadcrumbs
- 2 tsp dried tarragon
- 1 tsp parsley
- 1 tbsp unbleached flour
- 1/2 tsp salt
- 12 oz package frozen cauliflower florets, defrosted and drained
- Oil for misting

Instructions

Combine all the batter ingredients in a medium bowl, then put it aside. Place the breadcrumbs on a piece of wax paper. Combine the tarragon, parsley, flour, and salt in a small basin. To coat the cauliflower florets uniformly, stir the seasoning mixture into the vegetable. Use the batter to coat the cauliflower florets before coating them with breadcrumbs. Spray oil on all surfaces, then cook for 10 minutes at 390°F. Flip the florets, and cook for 5 minutes more or until they are golden and crispy.

Nutritional facts

Calories: 182, Carbohydrates: 5 g, Fat: 5 g, Protein: 4 g

5.7 Bell Pepper Rings

Preparation Time: 15 min

Cooking Time: 14 min

Servings: 4

Ingredients

- 2 bell peppers
- 1/2 cup all-purpose flour
- 1/2 teaspoon salt
- 1/2 cup lemon-lime soda
- 1/2 cup crushed panko breadcrumbs
- 1/2 cup plain breadcrumbs
- Cooking spray

Instructions

Set the air fryer to 390°F before using. Slice bell peppers into 1/4-inch rings. Remove the seeds and membranes. Mix the flour and salt in a large bowl. When the foaming stops and the mixture is medium-thick, slowly add the soda to the flour mixture while stirring. Stir the batter while adding the pepper rings, coating them completely. Put ordinary breadcrumbs and panko in a lidded plastic bag or container. Mix by shaking. Remove the pepper rings from the batter one at a time, shaking off the extra. Put the battered rings in the bag or container with the breadcrumbs. Lay the rings on a baking sheet or piece of wax paper after shaking to coat them. Bread all of the rings before spraying them with oil and place them in the air fryer basket. Stack the rings on top of each other, but be sure to leave plenty of space between them to allow air circulation while cooking. Cook for 10 minutes. Rearrange rings with tongs or a fork and spritz oil on any white areas. Cook for 3–4 minutes or until crispy and golden.

Nutritional facts

Calories: 183, Carbohydrates: 26 g, Fat: 5 g, Protein: 7 g

5.8 Cauliflower Spring Rolls with Peanut Sauce

Preparation Time: 20 min

Cooking Time: 20 min

Servings: 8 Spring Rolls

Ingredients

- 12 oz bag riced cauliflower, thawed
- 1/4 cup dried currants
- 1/4 cup coconut milk
- 1 tsp f curry powder
- 1/2 tsp cinnamon
- 2 tbsp minced green onions
- 1/4 tsp salt
- 8-inch rice paper wrappers
- Cooking spray
- 1/2 cup peanut butter
- 1 tbsp maple syrup
- 1 tbsp lemon or lime juice
- 1/2 tsp garlic powder
- 1 tbsp minced onion
- 1/4 tsp crushed red pepper flakes

Instructions

Combine the cauliflower rice, currants, coconut milk, curry powder, cinnamon, green onions, and salt in a big bowl. Cut the filling into 8 equal pieces. Dip quickly into lukewarm (about 105°F) water the rice paper wrapper to soften it. Place one part of the filling in the middle of the rice paper wrapper. Then, roll it up into a burrito by folding it in two of the sides. Discard on wax paper. Use three more sheets of rice paper and repeat the above steps. Place four spring rolls in the air fryer basket after spraying with cooking spray or oil on all sides. Cook for 10 minutes at 390°F. Cook for 10 more minutes on the other side until crisp and golden. Repeat the steps to prepare the second batch of spring rolls. Make the peanut sauce by blending or processing all of the sauce ingredients in a food processor until they are completely smooth while the spring rolls are cooking.

Nutritional facts

Calories: 182, Carbohydrates: 5 g, Fat: 3 g, Protein: 8 g

5.9 Cereal Snack Mix

Preparation Time: 5 min

Cooking Time: 7 min

Servings: 8

Ingredients

- 4 cups crispy rice cereal
- 1/4 tsp salt
- 2 tsp dill
- 3 tbsp grated Parmesan-style topping
- 1 tbsp soy sauce

Instructions

Stir all of the ingredients to coat them in a medium bowl thoroughly. Pour into the baking pan for the air fryer. Cook for 5 minutes at 360°F. Cook for 2 more minutes while stirring.

Nutritional facts

Calories: 238, Carbohydrates: 22 g, Fat: 15 g, Protein: 5 g

5.10 Cheddar-Olive Nuggets

Preparation Time: 20 min

Cooking Time: 15 min

Servings: 26 Nuggets

Ingredients

- 7 oz stuffed green olives
- 1 cup coconut yogurt
- 1 cup self-rising flour
- 1 tbsp all-vegetable shortening
- 3 tbsp almond milk
- Oil for mist over
- Strawberry Jam (non-compulsory)

Instructions

Drain the olives and dry them with paper towels. Use your hands to combine the flour and coconut yogurt. Incorporate the butter into the mixture, always with your hands, until it is well blended. Add the milk and stir until a dough forms. Roll the dough into a ball and then press the ball into a disc with a diameter of about 2 inches using 1 teaspoon of dough for each olive. Lay the olive in the middle of the dough, then encircle it while pinching and squeezing to seal it. Repeat to create 12 or 13 nuggets. The nuggets are sprayed with oil and arranged in a single layer in the air fryer basket. Cook for 13–15 minutes at 390°F or until golden. Repeat the above steps to cook the remaining nuggets. If desired, serve with strawberry jam for dipping.

Nutritional facts

Calories: 169, Carbohydrates: 23 g, Fat: 8 g, Protein: 5 g

5.11 Bitter Gourd Flat Cakes

Preparation Time: 5 min

Cooking Time: 20 min

Servings: 3

Ingredients

- 2 tbsp garam masala
- 2 cups sliced bitter gourd
- 3 tsp ginger finely chopped
- 2 tbsp fresh coriander leaves
- 3 green chilies, finely chopped
- 1 1/2 tbsp lemon juice
- Salt and pepper to taste

Instructions

In a fresh bowl, combine the ingredients and then pour in the water. Ensure the paste is thin enough to apply to the slices of bitter gourd and not too runny. Preheat the air fryer for 5 minutes at 160°F. The galettes should cook for an additional 25 minutes at the same temperature in the fry basket. Roll them over often to obtain a consistent cook. Serve with ketchup or mint chutney.

Nutritional facts

Calories: 145, Carbohydrates: 9.8 g, Fat: 10 g, Protein: 1.9 g

5.12 Chickpeas for Snacking

Preparation Time: 5 min

Cooking Time: 15 min

Servings: 1 Cup

Ingredients

- 15 oz can chickpeas, drained
- 2 tsp Tex-Mex Seasoning
- 1/4 tsp salt
- 1 tbsp olive oil

Instructions

Drain the chickpeas before spreading them out on a few paper towels in a single layer. Use another paper towel to cover. Roll and press lightly to wring out surplus moisture. Avoid pressing too firmly to avoid crushing the chickpeas. Put the chickpeas in a medium bowl with spices on top. Stir thoroughly to coat. Stir one more to properly spread the oil after adding. Cook for 12–15 minutes at 390°F while shaking the basket once halfway through. Store in an airtight jar after complete cooling.

Nutritional facts

Calories: 132, Carbohydrates: 14 g, Fat: 6 g, Protein: 5 g

5.13 Chickpea–Sweet Potato Croquettes

Preparation Time: 10 min

Cooking Time: 9 min

Servings: 12 croquettes

Ingredients

- 1 can chickpeas, worn out
- 1 tsp ground cumin
- 1/2 tsp ground coriander seed
- 1/2 tsp garlic powder
- 1/2 tsp onion powder
- 1/2 cup mashed sweet potatoes
- salt and pepper to taste
- 1/2 cup crushed panko breadcrumbs
- Cooking spray

Instructions

Set the air fryer to 390°F before using. Add half of the drained chickpeas to a food processor and the spices (cumin, coriander, garlic, and onion powder). Process the ingredients until it is almost entirely smooth. Place in a large bowl. Process the leftover chickpeas briefly enough to rough chop them. Don't go overboard— Leave some sizable portions. Add the chopped chickpeas to the bowl containing the plain chickpeas. Add the sweet potatoes and season to taste with salt and pepper. Make 12 croquettes out of the mixture, each measuring about 2 inches long. To ensure that they stay together, press them firmly. Mix the breadcrumbs and sesame seeds in a small bowl. Roll the croquettes in the crumb mixture and press down so that the coating sticks. Spray the croquettes lightly with oil and lay them out in a single layer in the air fryer basket. Then, close together without touching and cook for 7 minutes. Cook for another 2 minutes or until golden brown, misting any light areas that aren't browning.

Nutritional facts

Calories: 150, Carbohydrates: 160, Fat: 16 g, Protein: 15 g

5.14 Eggplant Fries with Curry Dip

Preparation Time: 10 min

Cooking Time: 8 min

Servings: 4

Ingredients

- 3/4 cup vegan mayonnaise
- 1 tsp curry powder
- 1/4 tsp dry mustard
- Black pepper to taste
- Hot sauce
- 2 tbsp Bob's Red Mill egg replacer
- 4 tbsp water
- 1 eggplant
- Salt to taste
- 1 cup crushed breadcrumbs
- 3 oz almond milk
- Cooking spray

Instructions

Combine all the dip components and blend well in a small bowl; cover and chill. Mix the egg substitute and water and set aside in a large dish. Peel the eggplant and cut it into 3/8- to 1-inch-thick fat fries. If you enjoy the flavor of the peel, keep it. Set the air fryer to 390°F before use. Add salt to taste to the fries. Put panko crumbs in a shallow dish. Whisk the milk into the egg mixture until thoroughly combined. Stir the egg wash into it before adding the eggplant fries. After brushing off the excess egg wash, remove the fries and coat them in breadcrumbs. Spray oil all over the fries. Put half of the fries in a single layer in the air fryer basket. The fries can somewhat crowd and encroach on one another. Cook for 5 minutes. Shake the basket, lightly spritz the fries once more with oil, and cook for 2–3 minutes until crispy and brown. Cook the remaining fries.

Nutritional facts

Calories: 130, Carbohydrates: 7 g, Fat: 2 g, Protein: 9 g

5.15 Granola

Preparation Time: 10 min

Cooking Time: 10 min

Servings: 2

Ingredients

- 1 cup rolled oats
- 1/4 cup shredded, unsweetened coconut
- 1/2 cup coarsely chopped walnuts
- 1/4 cup pumpkin seeds
- 2 tbsp sunflower seeds
- 1 tbsp flaxseed meal
- 1/2 cup dried cranberries
- 1/4 cup Date Paste
- 2 tbsp pure maple syrup
- 1 tsp vanilla extract
- Cooking spray

Instructions

Combine all dry ingredients in a large bowl. Date Paste, syrup, and vanilla should all be mixed together in a small basin. Pour the mixture of syrup over the dry ingredients. It is necessary to stir to coat the dry ingredients thoroughly. Apply a thin layer of oil or cooking spray to the air fryer baking pan. Place the granola in the pan and heat for 5 minutes at 390°F. Cook in 2 to 5 minutes batches, stirring every minute or so, until golden brown. Pay close attention because the mixture will cook quickly once it starts to brown. After removing it from the pan, spread the granola to cool on wax paper. After the granola is fully cooled, place it in an airtight container.

Nutritional facts

Calories: 167, Carbohydrates: 18 g, Fat: 9 g, Protein: 3 g

5.16 Jalapeño Poppers

Preparation Time: 1 hour

Cooking Time: 9 min

Servings: 20

Ingredients

- 4 oz vegan cream cheese
- 1 tsp grated lime zest
- 1/4 tsp chili powder
- 1/8 tsp garlic powder
- 1/4 tsp salt
- 1/2 lb jalapeño peppers
- 1 tbsp Bob's Red Mill egg replacer
- 1 tbsp lime juice
- 3 tbsp water
- 1/4 cup cornstarch
- 1/2 cup breadcrumbs
- 1/2 tsp salt
- Cooking spray

Instructions

Combine all the filling ingredients in a small bowl. While prepping the peppers, cover and place them in the fridge. Slice each jalapeño into a 1/2-inch thick piece. Remove the seeds and veins with a sharp knife, then discard, save for another use, or cut and incorporate into the filling for extra-hot poppers. Add filling to each pepper ring. Combine the egg substitute, lime juice, and water in a shallow dish. Put the corn flour in another small dish. Mix the salt and breadcrumbs in a third shallow dish. Coat each pepper slice in corn flour, shake off any excess, and then coat in the egg mixture. Press firmly to ensure that the breadcrumbs adhere as you roll the pepper slice in them. Freeze the pepper slices for 30 minutes after placing them in a single layer on a platter. Set the air fryer to 390°F before use. Spray the frozen peppers with oil or cooking spray, lay them out in a single layer in the air fryer basket, and cook for 5 minutes. Add a further 2−4 minutes cooking, or until the coating is browned and crispy, on any pieces that aren't browning.

Nutritional facts

Calories: 88, Carbohydrates: 4 g, Fat: 2 g, Protein: 3 g

5.17 Jalapeño-Tofu Sliders

Preparation Time: 15 min

Cooking Time: 7 min

Servings: 16 sliders

Ingredients

- 14 oz package firm silken tofu
- 1/2 cup bottled jalapeño slices
- 1/2 tsp salt
- 1/2 tsp onion powder
- 2 tbsp hot sauce
- 2 cups breadcrumbs, divided
- 3 tbsp potato starch
- Cooking spray
- 1/2 cup vegan sour cream
- 1/2 cup vegan mayonnaise
- 3 tbsp coarse brown mustard
- 2 tsp hot sauce
- 16 slider buns
- 4 small tomatoes, sliced
- Lettuce

Instructions

Set the air fryer to 390°F before use. Drain the tofu, dry it off, and then grate it into a large bowl. Mix thoroughly after adding the jalapeños, salt, onion powder, hot sauce, and 1 cup of panko. To help bind the mixture together, if necessary, whisk in the potato starch. When making the patties, they have to be moist but firm enough to maintain their shape. Place the remaining half cup of panko in a small dish. Form the tofu mixture into 16 slider-sized patties. Gently roll the patties in the panko, pressing just enough to help the coating adhere. Place 8 patties in the air fryer basket, mist with oil, and cook for 6–7 minutes, or until golden brown. Cook the remaining patties in the same manner. In the meantime, combine and thoroughly mix all the spread's components in a small bowl. Arrange the patties on warmed slider buns, and then top with spread, lettuce, and tomatoes to serve.

Nutritional facts

Calories: 134, Carbohydrates: 6.7 g, Fat: 9 g, Protein: 18 g

5.18 Mini Tacos

Preparation Time: 10 min

Cooking Time: 10 min

Servings: 24 mini tacos

Ingredients

- 24 corn tortillas
- 1 1/2 cups refried beans
- 1 small jar jalapeño slices
- 1 cup dairy-free sour cream
- cooking spray
- Sriracha sauce (non-compulsory)

Instructions

Set the air fryer to 390°F before use. Wrap the tortillas in wet paper towels and heat them on high for 30–60 seconds to soften them. Add 1 tablespoon of beans, 1 or 2 jalapeño slices, 1 tablespoon of dairy-free sour cream, and 1 teaspoon of salsa to each tortilla as you go. To seal the tortilla, fold it over, softly press down in the center, and then firmly press the edges all the way around. Apply cooking spray or oil to both sides. Put the air fryer basket with half the tacos inside. You may stand them upright and lean some against the sides to fit 12 in the basket. As long as there is some breathing room, crowding is acceptable. Cook for 8–10 minutes or until crispy and golden brown. Cooking the remaining tacos. Serve plain or with additional jalapeños and Sriracha sauce on top.

Nutritional facts

Calories: 150, Carbohydrates: 160, Fat: 16 g, Protein: 15 g

5.19 Pickled Okra Fries

Preparation Time: 10 min

Cooking Time: 12 min

Servings: 4 mini tacos

Ingredients

- 1 tbsp Bob's Red Mill egg replacer
- 2 tbsp water
- 16 oz jar pickled okra
- 1/2 cup panko breadcrumbs
- 1/2 cup Masa Harina flour
- 3 tbsp almond milk
- Cooking spray

Instructions

Combine the egg replacer and water in a large mixing dish large enough to handle all of the okra. Allow to thicken. Clean the okra and slice each pod lengthwise in half. Put the panko and Masa Harina in a large plastic bag or lidded container. Shake or whisk to thoroughly combine. Heat the air fryer to 390°F. Until smooth, mix the almond milk into the egg mixture. Stir gently to coat the okra with the egg wash. Remove the okra from the egg wash, allowing any excess to drain. Shake the okra slices in the panko mixture to coat. Place the fried okra in the air fryer basket and coat it with cooking spray or oil. 5 minutes in the oven.

Shake the basket to reposition the pieces, then spray with more oil or frying spray and cook for 5 minutes more. Shake to separate any stuck-together okra bits. Spray again to cover any areas you missed. Cook for another 1–2 minutes, or until lightly browned and crispy.

Nutritional facts

Calories: 113, Carbohydrates: 16 g, Fat: 1.2 g, Protein: 1.9 g

5.20 Pita Chips

Preparation Time: 5 min

Cooking Time: 6 min

Servings: 4

Ingredients

- 2 (6 inches) pitas
- 1 1/4 tsp Tex-Mex Seasoning
- 1/4 tsp salt
- Cooking spray

Instructions

Cut each pita half into 4 wedges. Split the wedges at the fold to make 32 chips in total. Combine the Tex-Mex spice and salt in a small bowl. Spray one side of the chips with oil, then top with half of the seasoning mix. Turn the chips over, spray with oil, and season with the remaining seasoning. Put the pita chips in the air fryer basket and cook for 2 minutes at 330°F. Cook for 2 minutes more after shaking the basket. Shake again and heat for another 1–2 minutes or until crisp. To avoid burning, keep a close eye on the situation.

Nutritional facts

Calories: 136, Carbohydrates: 16 g, Fat: 7 g, Protein: 3 g

5.21 Potato Chips

Preparation Time: 15 min

Cooking Time: 15 min

Servings: 3

Ingredients

- 2 potatoes
- 2 tsp vegan oil
- Salt and pepper to taste
- Cooking spray

Instructions

Peel the potatoes. If desired, the peel can be left on. Shave the potatoes into extremely thin slices with a mandolin, putting them into a water dish as you go. Dry the slices well with paper towels or a clean dish towel. Toss the potato pieces in the oil to coat thoroughly. Spray the air fryer basket with cooking spray or oil. Stir in the potatoes with a fork to break up the slices. Cook for 5 minutes at 390°F. Break apart and stir. Cook for 5 minutes more. Stir once more to separate. Cook for another 5 minutes or until crispy. Season with salt and pepper to taste.

Nutritional facts

Calories: 370, Carbohydrates: 49 g, Fat: 16 g, Protein: 5 g

5.22 Roasted Nuts

Preparation Time: 1 min

Cooking Time: 7 min

Servings: 1 cup

Ingredients

- 1 cup blanched whole almonds

Instructions

Heat your air fryer to 360°F. Fill the air fryer basket halfway with nuts. Cook for 3 minutes with the nuts. Come to a halt and jiggle the basket. Cook for another 2–4 minutes, or until the nuts are golden to your taste.

Nutritional facts

Calories: 178, Carbohydrates: 10 g, Fat: 14 g, Protein: 6 g

5.23 Smoky Sandwich

Preparation Time: 5 min

Cooking Time: 8 min

Servings: 2 Sandwiches

Ingredients

- 4 pieces whole-grain bread
- 4 pieces vegan cheese

- 2 pieces meatless hickory-smoked deli slices
- Olive to spray

Instructions

On a chopping board, place 2 slices of bread. Place on top of each slice of bread 1 piece of vegan cheese, 1 slice of cold meat, the other portion of cheese, and finally the other slice of bread. Brush oil on both sides of the sandwich. Divide each sandwich into 2 rectangular halves. Place the bread in the air fryer basket and cook at 390°F for 5–8 minutes, or until it toasts.

Nutritional facts

Calories: 261, Carbohydrates: 12 g, Fat: 5 g, Protein: 4 g

5.24 Spinach-Artichoke Dip

Preparation Time: 17 min

Cooking Time: 12 min

Servings: 2 cups

Ingredients

- 1 cup ice-covered spinach
- 1/3 cup vegan tart cream
- 1/4 cup vegan mayonnaise
- 1 tbsp fresh squeezed lime juice
- 3 tbsp sliced green onions
- 1 cup canned artichoke hearts
- Cooking spray
- Crackers for serving

Instructions

Thaw the spinach and wring away any extra liquid. Combine the vegan sour cream, vegan mayonnaise, and lime juice in a medium mixing bowl. Stir in the green onions, spinach, and artichoke hearts until well combined. Spray your baking pan with oil or cooking spray and spoon the mixture into it. Sauté at 360°F for 10–12 minutes or until the dip is well heated. With a little toast or crackers, serve the dip warm.

Nutritional facts

Calories: 50, Carbohydrates: 1 g, Fat: 3 g, Protein: 1 g

5.25 String Bean Fries

Preparation Time: 15 min

Cooking Time: 6 min

Servings: 4

Ingredients

- 1/2 lb fresh string beans
- 2 tbsp Bob's Red Mill egg replacer
- 1/2 cup water
- 1/2 cup white flour
- 1/2 cup breadcrumbs
- 1/4 tsp salt
- 1/4 tsp grounded black pepper
- 1/4 tsp dry mustard
- Cooking spray

Instructions

Preheat the air fryer to 360°F. Trim the green beans' stem ends, then wash and pat them dry. Mix the egg replacer and water in a shallow dish until well combined. Place the flour in a separate shallow dish. Combine the breadcrumbs, salt, pepper, and dry mustard in a third shallow dish. Dip each string bean in the egg mixture, flour, egg mixture again, and breadcrumbs one at a time. When you've coated all the string beans, open the air fryer and drop them in the basket. Cook for 3 minutes. Cook for 2–3 minutes more or until the string beans are brown and crisp.

Nutritional facts

Calories: 60, Carbohydrates: 10 g, Fat: 7 g, Protein: 6 g

5.26 Stuffed Dates

Preparation Time: 15 min

Cooking Time: 5 min

Servings: 12 Dates

Ingredients

- 4 1/2 tsp Bob's Red Mill egg replacer, separated
- 5 tbsp water, divided
- 12 Medjool dates
- 1/4 cup sliced almonds
- 1/4 cup shredded unsweetened coconut
- 1/4 tsp almond extract
- 2 tbsp cornstarch
- 1/2 cup crushed panko breadcrumbs
- Cooking spray

Instructions

Set aside 1 1/2 teaspoons of the egg replacer and 3 tablespoons of water in a small mixing basin. Cut a lengthwise slit in each date, remove the pit, and spread the date open slightly. Combine the nuts, coconut, almond extract, and 1 tablespoon of egg wash in a food processor. Short pulses are enough to finely chop the nuts and mix the ingredients. Add the remaining 3 teaspoons of egg replacer and 3 tablespoons of water to the remaining egg wash. Mix thoroughly with a whisk. Put the corn flour in one shallow dish and the breadcrumbs in another. Preheat the air fryer to 390°F. Fill each date with the nut mixture, pressing down firmly. Fill the dates until the point where the slits are slightly open. Tap off any extra corn flour from each date. Dip each date in the egg wash and then roll in the crumbs. Spray the dates with oil, and then place them in the air fryer basket for 3 minutes. Mist with oil again and heat for 1–2 minutes more or until the outer layer browns and becomes crispy.

Nutritional facts

Calories: 555, Carbohydrates: 90 g, Fat: 15 g, Protein: 23 g

5.27 Sweet Potato Fries

Preparation Time: 15 min

Cooking Time: 15 min

Servings: 4

Ingredients

- 3 sweet potatoes
- 1 tbsp light olive oil
- 1 tbsp dried tarragon
- Salt and pepper to taste
- Cinnamon sugar (non-compulsory)

Instructions

Cut the sweet potatoes into 14 x 3-inch fries. (Optional: peel the potatoes.) Toss the fries with the oil and tarragon to coat completely. Place the fries in the air fryer basket and cook for 5 minutes at 390°F. Cook for 5 minutes more, stirring or shaking the basket, until the fries are golden. Season with salt and pepper or cinnamon sugar to suit.

Nutritional facts

Calories: 370, Carbohydrates: 49 g, Fat: 16 g, Protein: 5 g

5.28 Texas Toothpicks

Preparation Time: 25 min

Cooking Time: 14 min

Servings: 4

Ingredients

- 1 lb jalapeño peppers
- 1/2 cup all-purpose flour
- 1/2 cup crushed breadcrumbs
- 1/2 tsp smoked paprika
- 1/2 tsp onion powder
- 1/2 tsp salt
- 1/2 cup potato starch
- 1/2 cup almond milk
- Cooking spray

Instructions

Wash the jalapeños and cut them in half lengthwise while using food-grade gloves. Discard the seeds, membranes, and stalks from the plant.

Cut them into 1/4-inch-long slivers at their widest point. Preheat the air fryer to 390°F. Combine the flour, breadcrumbs, paprika, onion powder, and salt in a plastic bag or a container with a lid. Shake well to combine. In one small bowl, combine the potato starch and the almond milk. Dredge the pepper strips in the potato starch to coat them, working with approximately a third of them at a time. Shake off any extra starch before dipping them in the milk and allowing the excess to drop off. Shake the breadcrumbs over the jalapeño slivers to coat, and then spread them out on a cookie or baking sheet. Mist the slivers with oil once you've finished coating them. To cook the slivers in the air fryer basket all at once, arrange crisscross layers so that air circulates, and the strips don't cling together. Cook for 5 minutes in the oven. Gently shake or stir and spritz with oil. Cook for 5 minutes more. Cook for 2–4 minutes longer or until the slivers turn golden brown, stirring occasionally.

Nutritional facts

Calories: 120, Carbohydrates: 24 g, Fat: 1.5 g, Protein: 3 g

5.29 Tomato-Caprese Cups

Preparation Time: 12 min

Cooking Time: 5 min

Servings: 15 pieces

Ingredients

- 1 cup vegan mozzarella
- 15-count package mini phyllo cups
- 1 tbsp dried basil
- 15 slices black olives
- 8 grape tomatoes
- Oil for mist over

Instructions

Coarsely cut the vegan mozzarella pieces and divide evenly between the phyllo cups. Spread the basil on top of the cheese. Put 1 black olive slice on top of each. Cut the tomatoes in half lengthwise. In each cup, place 1 tomato half cut side down. Spray the cups using oil. Fill the air fryer basket halfway with the cups. You can fit them all on one layer. Cook for 5 minutes at 390°F to melt the cheese. Serve hot.

Nutritional facts

Calories: 211, Carbohydrates: 14 g, Fat: 6 g, Protein: 6 g

5.30 Tortilla Strips

Preparation Time: 5 min

Cooking Time: 7 min

Servings: 4 Servings

Ingredients

- 10 (8-inch) corn tortillas
- Oil for mist over

Instructions

Mist each tortilla with oil, front and back, and then stack. Make 1⁄4 x 1-1⁄2 inch strips out of the tortillas. Place all of the pieces in the air fryer basket and cook for 5 minutes at 390°F. Cook for 2 minutes more, stirring occasionally, until they are golden and crisp.

Nutritional facts

Calories: 67, Carbohydrates: 12 g, Fat: 2 g, Protein: 1 g

5.31 Tuscan Tomato Toast

Preparation Time: 5 min

Cooking Time: 8 min

Servings: 2 Toasts

Ingredients

- 1 tsp virgin olive oil
- 1 tsp Tuscan Herb Mix
- 2 slices Italian-style bread, cut to 1⁄2 x 3 x 6 inches
- 1/2 cup sundried tomatoes, torn
- 1 slice vegan provolone cheese

Instructions

Combine the olive oil and Tuscan Herb Mix in a small mixing bowl. Brush one side of the toast with the seasoned oil. Cover every unoiled side of the bread with sundried tomatoes and cover with cheese. Cook at 390°F for 5–8 minutes, until the bottom of the bread is toasted, and the cheese melts.

Nutritional facts

Calories: 211, Carbohydrates: 14 g, Fat: 6 g, Protein: 6 g

Chapter 6: Desserts

6.1 Amaretto Poached Pears

Preparation Time: 10 min

Cooking Time: 15 min

Servings: 4

Ingredients

- 1/2 cup of amaretto liqueur
- 1/2 cup of water
- 2 fresh pears

Instructions

Combine the olive oil and Tuscany Herb Mix in a small mixing bowl. Brush one side of the toast with the seasoned oil. Cover every unoiled side of the bread with sundried tomatoes and cover with cheese. Cook for 5-8 minutes until the bottom of the bread is toasted and the cheese melts at 390°F.

Nutritional facts

Calories: 384, Carbohydrates: 74 g, Fat: 1 g, Protein: 1 g

6.2 Apple Pies

Preparation Time: 30 min

Cooking Time: 20 min

Servings: 12 pies

Ingredients

- 2 cups self-rising flour, separated
- 1/4 cup all-vegetable shortening
- 3/4 cup almond milk
- 4 cups peeled, cored, and diced apples
- 1 tbsp lemon juice
- 1 cup sugar
- 1 tbsp cornstarch
- 1 tsp cinnamon oil for misting

Instructions

Place 2 cups of flour in a medium mixing bowl. Cut the shortening into the flour using a pastry blender. Set the dough aside while you prepare the apples and stir in the almond milk. Dice the apples into 1/4-inch pieces to prevent browning, and place them in another medium bowl. Add the lemon juice and mix to coat evenly. Combine the sugar, corn flour, and cinnamon in a small bowl. Stir the dry ingredients into the apples to coat. On a sheet of wax paper, sprinkle the remaining 1/4 cup flour. Make 12 equal-sized balls out of the dough. Roll each ball into a thin circle about 5 inches in diameter on floured wax paper. Spoon 1 1/2 tablespoons apple filling onto one side of a dough circle. Moisten the inside border of the dough circle all around with a finger dipped in water. Fold the dough in half to form a half-moon, then seal and crimp the edges with a fork. Repeat the above steps with 3 more rings of dough. After misting both sides with oil or cooking spray, place the pies in the air fryer basket. Bake 4 pies at a time at 360°F for 18–20 minutes, or until light golden brown. Make the remaining pies while each batch is cooking.

Nutritional facts

Calories: 57, Carbohydrates: 6 g, Fat: 2 g, Protein: 3 g

6.3 Apple Wedgies

Preparation Time: 10 min

Cooking Time: 5 min

Servings: 4

Ingredients

- 1 tbsp Bob's Red Mill egg replacer
- 5 tbsp water
- 1/4 cup panko breadcrumbs
- 1/4 cup chopped peanuts
- 1 tsp coconut sugar
- 1 tsp cocoa powder
- 1 tsp cinnamon
- 1/4 cup potato starch
- Cooking spray

Instructions

Set aside the egg replacer and water in a shallow dish to thicken. Combine the breadcrumbs, peanuts, sugar, and salt in a separate shallow dish. Add the cinnamon and chocolate. Place the potato starch in a resalable plastic bag or a container with a lid. Preheat the air fryer to 390°F. Make tiny slices out of the apple. The thickest edge should be no thicker than 3/8–1/2 inch. Remove the core but do not peel. Shake the apple wedges in the potato starch to coat. Roll the wedges in the crumb mixture after dipping them in the egg wash. Spray the wedges with oil or cooking spray, set them in a single layer in the air fryer basket, and cook for 5 minutes until brown and crispy. The chocolate will darken the coating, but the peanut bits will turn golden brown. Serve immediately.

Nutritional facts

Calories: 187, Carbohydrates: 20 g, Fat: 9 g, Protein: 7 g

6.4 Baked Apples

Preparation Time: 10 min

Cooking Time: 20 min

Servings: 6 apple halves

Ingredients

- Baking apples
- 3 tbsp chopped pecans
- 3 tbsp pure maple syrup
- 1 tbsp vegan butter, divided

Instructions

Fill the air fryer drawer with 1/2 cup of water. Wash and pat dry the apples before cutting them in half. Core the halves and scoop out about 1 tablespoon of apple flesh to create a hollow for the pecans. Place the apple halves in the air fryer basket with the cut side up. Spoon 1 teaspoon of pecans and 1/2 tablespoon of maple syrup into each apple cavity. Spread half a teaspoon of vegan butter on each apple half. Cook for 20 minutes at 360°F or until the apples are soft and tender.

Nutritional facts

Calories: 57, Carbohydrates: 6 g, Fat: 2 g, Protein: 3 g

6.5 Banana Bread Pudding

Preparation Time: 10 min

Cooking Time: 20 min

Servings: 6

Ingredients

- 1 tbsp Bob's Red Mill egg replacer
- 2 tbsp water cooking spray
- 1 cup all-purpose flour
- 1 tsp baking powder
- 1/4 tsp salt
- 1/4 cup mashed ripe banana

- 1/4 cup peanut butter
- 1/4 cup almond milk
- 1/4 cup pure maple syrup
- 2 tbsp coconut oil
- 1/2 tsp pure vanilla extract

Instructions

Mix the egg replacer and water in a small bowl and put aside for 1 minute to thicken. Heat the air fryer to 330°F. Lightly coat a 6 × 6-inch baking dish with cooking spray. Combine the flour, baking powder, and salt in a medium mixing basin. Blend the banana, peanut butter, milk, maple syrup, coconut oil, vanilla, and egg mixture in a separate mixing dish and blend well. Stir the banana mixture into the dry ingredients gently. Blend thoroughly but do not beat. The batter will be quite thick. Cook for 20–22 minutes, spreading the batter equally in the prepared baking dish. It is done when the top of the pudding has been browned and feels solid when touched with the back of a spoon.

Nutritional facts

Calories: 383, Carbohydrates: 47 g, Fat: 20 g, Protein: 7 g

6.6 Cherry-Berry Crisp

Preparation Time: 10 min

Cooking Time: 9 min

Servings: 4

Ingredients

- Cooking spray
- 10 oz bag frozen cherries
- 1 cup new blueberries
- 1/4 cup coconut sugar
- 2 tbsp amaretto liqueur
- 2 tbsp oats
- 2 tbsp oat bran
- 1/4 cup cooked quinoa
- 2 tbsp almonds
- 2 tbsp coconut sugar
- 2 tsp coconut oil

Instructions

Preheat the air fryer to 360°F. Spray the non-stick cooking spray on the air fryer baking pan. In the baking pan, combine all of the filling ingredients and stir thoroughly. Combine all the topping ingredients in a medium mixing bowl and stir until the oil is equally distributed and the mixture is crumbly. Spread the topping equally on top of the contents in the pan. Cook for 7–9 minutes until the crumbs are golden brown and crispy.

Nutritional facts

Calories: 553, Carbohydrates: 82 g, Fat: 24 g, Protein: 4 g

6.7 Chocolate Cake

Preparation Time: 10 min

Cooking Time: 30 min

Servings: 8

Ingredients

- Cooking spray
- 1 tbsp of Bob's Red Mill egg replacer
- 2 tbsp water
- 1/2 cup sugar
- 1/4 cup self-rising flour, plus
- 3 tbsp cocoa
- 1/4 tsp baking soda
- 1/4 tsp salt
- 2 tbsp vegan oil
- 5 (3 oz) containers vegan vanilla yogurt
- 1/4 cup nut milk of choice

Instructions

Preheat the air fryer to 330°F. Set aside the baking pan sprayed with oil/cooking spray. Whisk together the egg replacer and water in a medium mixing basin using a wire whisk. Whisk in the remaining ingredients until smooth. Cook for 25–30 minutes, or until a toothpick put into the middle comes out clean, in the air fryer baking pan. Allow the cake to cool in the pan for 10 minutes before lifting it.

Nutritional facts

Calories: 366, Carbohydrates: 56 g, Fat: 14 g, Protein: 5 g

6. 8 Coconut Pound Cake with Pineapple-Lime Topping

Preparation Time: 10 min

Cooking Time: 35 min

Servings: 8

Ingredients

- Cooking spray
- 1 tbsp Bob's Red Mill egg replacer
- 2 tbsp water
- 1/2 cup sugar
- 1 1/2 cups self-rising flour
- 2 tbsp coconut oil
- 1 cup coconut milk
- 1/2 cup unsweetened flaked coconut
- 1 8-oz can pineapple in juice, crushed
- 1 tsp grated lime zest
- 1 tbsp lime juice
- 1 cup sugar

Instructions

Preheat the air fryer to 330°F. Set aside the air fryer baking pan sprayed with nonstick spray. Whisk both the egg replacer and water in a medium mixing basin using a wire whisk. Whisk in the sugar, flour, coconut oil, and coconut milk until well combined. Incorporate the coconut. Cook for 30–35 minutes, or until a toothpick stuck into the middle comes out with soft crumbs attached, in the preheated pan. Allow the cake to cool for 10 minutes in the pan before removing it. Prepare the topping while the cake is baking. Mix all of the topping components in a small saucepan over medium-high heat. Bring the topping to a boil while constantly stirring for 1 minute, then removes from the heat. Allow the topping to cool before serving at room temperature.

Nutritional facts

Calories: 190, Carbohydrates: 28 g, Fat: 8 g, Protein: 2 g

6.9 Dundee Cake

Preparation Time: 16 min

Cooking Time: 30 min

Servings: 8

Ingredients

- Cooking spray
- 2 tbsp Bob's Red Mill egg replacer
- 4 tbsp water
- 4 tbsp coconut oil
- 1/2 cup sugar
- 1 cup dried currants
- 1/3 cup slivered almonds
- 1 tbsp grated orange peel
- 1 tbsp grated lemon peel
- 1 cup self-rising flour
- 1/2 cup almond flour
- 2 tbsp orange juice

Instructions

Coat the air fryer baking pan with nonstick cooking spray. Heat the air fryer to 330°F. In a large mixing basin, combine the egg replacer and water. Mix in the coconut oil and sugar until smooth. Combine the flours, almonds, currants, lemon and orange peels, and orange juice, liqueur, or brandy. Smooth the batter into the air fryer baking pan. Cook for 30 minutes, till a toothpick stuck into the center comes out with moist crumbs.

Nutritional facts

Calories: 384, Carbohydrates: 56 g, Fat: 15 g, Protein: 5 g

6.10 Peach-Fried Pies

Preparation Time: 30 min

Cooking Time: 20 min

Servings: 12 Pies

Ingredients

- 2 cups self-rising flour
- 1/4 cup all-vegetable shortening
- 1/4 cup almond milk,
- 1/4 cup sugar
- 1 tbsp cornstarch
- 3 1/2 cups diced fresh peaches
- 1/2 cup dried cherries
- 1/2 cup o sliced almonds
- 1 tbsp lemon juice
- 1/2 cup all-purpose white flour for the work surface
- Cooking spray

Instructions

Combine the flour and shortening with a pastry blender in a large mixing bowl. Set aside after stirring in the almond milk until a soft dough forms. Set aside the ingredients for the filling in a separate bowl. Divide the dough into 12 equal-sized pieces and roll into balls. Sprinkle one tablespoon of flour on a sheet of wax paper. Roll out one dough ball to a 5-inch diameter circle on wax paper dusted with flour. To keep the dough from sticking, add more flour as needed. Spread a heaping dollop of filling on top of the dough. Moisten the inside edge of the dough with a pastry brush, or your finger dipped in water. Fold the dough over to form a half-moon shape, press to close, and crimp the sides tight with a fork. Make 3 more pies. After misting both sides with oil or cooking spray, place the pies in the air fryer basket. Cook at 360°F for 18–20 minutes or until the crust is gently browned.

Nutritional facts

Calories: 258, Carbohydrates: 35 g, Fat: 12 g, Protein: 3 g

6.11 Peach Pudding Cake

Preparation Time: 10 min

Cooking Time: 35 min

Servings: 8

Ingredients

- 1 8-oz can peaches, diced, packed in juice
- Cooking spray
- 1 tbsp Bob's Red Mill egg replacer
- 2 tbsp water
- 1 cup self-rising flour
- 1/4 tsp baking soda
- 1/2 cup sugar
- 2 tbsp oil
- 5 (3 oz) containers vegan peach yogurt
- 1/4 cup almond milk
- 1/4 tsp almond extract

Instructions

Preheat the air fryer to 330°F. Place the drained peaches in a single layer on several paper towels and top with more paper towels to remove excess moisture. Spray the air fryer baking pan with cooking spray or oil. Mix the egg replacer and water in a medium dish with a wire whisk. Whisk in the other ingredients, including the peaches, until completely combined. Cook for 35 minutes, or until a toothpick pushed into the center of the cake comes out clean, in the air fryer baking pan. Allow the cake to cool for 10 minutes before removing it from the pan.

Nutritional facts

Calories: 383, Carbohydrates: 47 g, Fat: 20 g, Protein: 7 g

6.12 Peaches Poached in Raspberry Syrup

Preparation Time: 20 min

Cooking Time: 15 min

Servings: 6

Ingredients

- 6 oz package frozen raspberries, thawed
- 1/2 cup sugar
- 5 cups water, divided (room temperature)
- 2 lb fresh peaches
- 1 tbsp lemon juice

Instructions

Combine the raspberries, sugar, and a half cup of water in a small saucepan over medium-high heat. Bring the raspberries to a boil and cook until the sugar has dissolved. Prepare the peaches while the raspberry syrup is heating. Pour 4 cups of water and the lemon juice into a large mixing basin. Cut a deep slice from the stem to the peach blossom end, close to the pit. Turn the peach over and make the same cut on the opposite side. Cut each of those 2 slices in half lengthwise. Cut slices from the peach's 2 remaining sides. Place the peach slices in a dish of water after peeling them. Drain the peaches and place them in the baking pan of the air fryer. Pour over the peaches the boiling raspberry syrup. Cook for 10 minutes at 360°F. Cook for another 5 minutes, stirring occasionally.

Allow to cool to lukewarm before chilling if desired.

Nutritional facts

Calories: 258, Carbohydrates: 35 g, Fat: 12 g, Protein: 3 g

6.13 Strawberry Sauce

Preparation Time: 10 min

Cooking Time: 15 min

Servings: 8

Ingredients

- 1 lb fresh strawberries
- 1/2 tsp grated orange rind
- 1 tsp orange liqueur
- 1/2 cup sugar

Instructions

Mix all the strawberries, orange rind, orange liqueur, and sugar in an air fryer baking pan. Cook for 5 minutes at 390°F. Cook for another 10 minutes, stirring occasionally.

Nutritional facts

Calories: 106, Carbohydrates: 26 g, Fat: 18 g, Protein: 1 g

Chapter 7: Salads

7.2 Corn Salad

Preparation Time: 6 min

Cooking Time: 18 min

Servings: 12

Ingredients

- 1 tbsp light olive oil
- 1/2 tsp garlic powder
- 1/2 tsp cumin
- 2 slight corn ears
- 1 cup cooked black beans
- 1/2 cup slivered poblano peppers
- 1/2 onion
- 1 avocado
- 3 tbsp lime juice
- 1/4 teaspoon salt

Instructions

Combine the olive oil, garlic powder, and cumin in a small bowl. Remove the corn husk and silk from the ears. Brush the oil mixture over all of the corn's surfaces. Place the corn in the air fryer basket and cook for 10–12 minutes at 390°F. While the corn is cooking, cut the poblano peppers into about 1/8-inch broad slivers and cube the onion. When the corn is done, set it on a chopping board, stem end down, and slice or scrape the kernels from the cobs. Cut the avocado into 1/4-inch chunks. Toss the corn, beans, peppers, onion, and avocado with the lime juice and salt.

Nutritional facts

Calories: 209, Carbohydrates: 36 g, Fat: 7 g, Protein: 7 g

7.3 Crabless Salad with Pineapple Salsa

Preparation Time: 10 min

Cooking Time: 10 min

Servings: 4

Ingredients

- 10 8-oz packages crabless cakes
- oil to spray
- 1 cup crushed pineapple
- 1/3 cup crushed red onion
- 1/3 cup crushed bell pepper, any color
- 4 cups shredded cabbage

Instructions

Place the crab cakes in the air fryer basket and coat all sides with oil or cooking spray. Cook for 10 minutes at 390°F or until they are brown and crisp. In the meantime, combine the pineapple, red onion, and bell pepper for the salsa. Put 1 cup of shredded cabbage on each of the 4 salad dishes. Distribute the salsa equally on top of the cabbage. To serve, arrange 5 baked cakes on each platter.

Nutritional facts

Calories: 200, Carbohydrates: 31 g, Fat: 8 g, Protein: 8 g

7.1 Broccoli-Tofu Salad

Preparation Time: 50 min

Cooking Time: 20 min

Servings: 4

Ingredients

- 4 oz extra-firm tofu
- 1 tsp smoked paprika
- 1 tsp onion powder
- 1/4 tsp salt
- 2 tbsp cornstarch
- 1 tbsp extra-virgin olive oil
- 4 cups fresh broccoli
- 1/2 chopped cup red onion
- 1/3 cup raisins or dried cherries
- 3/4 cup sliced almonds

- 1/2 cup Asian-style salad dressing

Instructions

To begin, drain the tofu. If you possess a tofu press, put it in it and press for 30 minutes before proceeding to the next step. If not, place many folded paper towels on a dish. Place the tofu on top, then cover with folded paper towels and a platter. Fill it with cans or other stuff to make it heavier. Press the tofu should for 30 minutes. While the tofu drains, combine all the salad ingredients in a large mixing dish. Chill covered. Cut the drained tofu block into 1/4-inch thick cubes. Combine the smoked paprika, onion powder, and salt in a small bowl. Sprinkle the smoked paprika mixture over both sides of the tofu cubes. Shake the corn flour and tofu in a small plastic bag or container with a lid to coat. Shake the olive oil and covered tofu cubes in another small plastic bag or container and coat well. Cook for 17–20 minutes at 330°F or until the cubes are as crispy as desired. To serve, toss the salad with the dressing, divide it among serving dishes, and top with the cooked tofu.

Nutritional facts

Calories: 174, Carbohydrates: 7 g, Fat: 9 g, Protein: 18 g

7.4 Portabella Salad

Preparation Time: 15 min

Cooking Time: 10 min

Servings: 2

Ingredients

- 6 oz portabella mushroom caps
- 1 tbsp vegan Worcestershire sauce
- 1/4 tsp dry mustard
- 1/4 tsp lemon juice black pepper
- 1 tbsp extra-light olive oil,
- 6 tbsp vegan mayonnaise
- 1 tbsp almond milk
- 2 tsp prepared horseradish
- 1/2 tsp coarse brown mustard
- 1/2 tsp vegan Worcestershire sauce

- 4 cups romaine lettuce

Instructions

Remove the mushroom stems and discard. Remove the gills and clean the mushroom caps. Mix the vegan Worcestershire sauce, mustard, lemon juice, pepper, and oil in a small bowl to prepare a marinade. Combine thoroughly. Brush the mushroom tops with the marinade. Turn the mushrooms over and liberally cover the stem sides with marinade. Place the stem side up in the air fryer basket. If necessary, stack them slightly or lean them against the basket's sides, but leave some room between them. Cook for 5 minutes at 360°F. Cook for 5 minutes more or until the mushrooms are done. Make the salad dressing while the mushrooms are cooking. Blend all dressing ingredients in a small bowl, whisk to blend, and refrigerate until ready to serve. Make bite-size chunks out of the mushrooms. Distribute the greens, tomatoes, and onion slivers across 2 dishes. Serve with the mushroom bits and salad dressing at the table.

Nutritional facts

Calories: 213, Carbohydrates: 21 g, Fat: 9 g, Protein: 13 g

7.5 Potato Salad with Asparagus

Preparation Time: 15 min

Cooking Time: 12 min

Servings: 8

Ingredients

- 3 Yukon Gold potatoes
- 1 tbsp light olive oil
- 1/2 tsp thyme
- 1 1/2 cups of asparagus
- 1/2 medium onion
- salt and pepper to taste
- 1 tbsp light olive oil
- 2 tbsp balsamic vinegar
- 1 tbsp Dijon mustard

Instructions

Scrub the potatoes under cool running water with a vegetable brush. Dice the potatoes into 34-inch chunks. Toss the potatoes in the oil and thyme mixture in a medium bowl. Place the potatoes in the air fryer basket, leaving the oil and mixing bowl aside for later. Cook potatoes for 6 minutes at 390°F. While the potatoes are cooking, thinly slice the onions and cut the asparagus into 3-inch pieces. Toss the asparagus and onions in the remaining oil in the mixing dish. Combine the breaded asparagus, onions, and potatoes in the air fryer. Cook for another 6 minutes. While the vegetables are cooking, prepare the balsamic dressing by whisking together the dressing ingredients in a small bowl. Toss the warm vegetables with the balsamic dressing and set aside to cool to room temperature, stirring occasionally. Season to taste with salt and pepper.

Nutritional facts

Calories: 130, Carbohydrates: 21 g, Fat: 5 g, Protein: 3 g

7.6 Tofu Napa Salad

Preparation Time: 10 min

Cooking Time: 10 min

Servings: 4

Ingredients

- 14 oz firm tofu, pressed
- 3 tbsp cornstarch
- Oil for mist over
- 1/2 tsp smoked paprika
- 1/4 tsp salt
- 1/4 tsp garlic powder
- 1/2 tsp onion powder
- 1/8 tsp ginger
- 1 tbsp extra-light olive oil
- 1 tbsp coconut sugar
- 2 tbsp red wine vinegar
- 2 tbsp coarse brown mustard
- 3 tbsp extra-light olive oil
- 1/4 sweet red bell pepper

- 1 Granny Smith apple
- 8 cups shredded Napa cabbage

Instructions

Cut the tofu into 12-inch chunks. Place the tofu in a plastic bag or a small container with a cover. Mix the marinade ingredients in a small basin, and pour over the tofu cubes. Refrigerate for a minimum of 30 minutes and up to 24 hours. Preheat the air fryer to 390°F when ready to cook. Shake the corn flour and marinated tofu cubes in a separate plastic bag or container with a lid to coat lightly. Cook for 5 minutes after placing the tofu cubes in the air fryer basket and misting them with oil. Shake the basket to redistribute the cubes, then re-mist with oil and fry for 5 minutes more. Place the cubes on a plate to cool for a few minutes. Make the dressing while the tofu is cooking. Dissolve the sugar in the vinegar in a jar or cruet. Shake vigorously to combine the remaining dressing ingredients. Sliver the red bell pepper, then core, 1/4, and cut the apple crosswise into pieces. Toss the cabbage, bell pepper slivers, apple slices, and dressing in a large mixing basin. Distribute the salad mixture among four dishes and top with tofu.

Nutritional facts

Calories: 174, Carbohydrates: 7 g, Fat: 9 g, Protein: 18 g

7.7 Warm Fruit Salad

Preparation Time: 10 min

Cooking Time: 10 min

Servings: 6

Ingredients

- 1/3 cup coconut chips
- 1/3 cup chopped walnuts
- Oil for mist over
- 1 cup frozen pineapple, thawed
- 1 cup frozen peaches, thawed
- 15 oz can dark, sweet pitted cherries, drained
- 1/4 tsp brandy extract
- 1 banana

- 2 tbsp dried cranberries

Instructions

Preheat the air fryer to 390°F. Mix the coconut chips and walnuts in the air fryer baking pan, spritz with oil, and stir. Brown for 1–2 minutes. Take your time! In 30 seconds or less, coconut can transform from golden brown to charred black. To avoid overcooking, pause your air fryer and inspect it periodically. Set the topping aside after removing it from the baking pan. Combine the pineapple, peaches, cherries, and brandy flavoring in the same baking dish. Cook for 4 minutes with the fruit combination. Cook for 2 minutes more, stirring occasionally. Slice the banana and add it to the fruit mixture. Cook for another 2 minutes or until the banana is warm. When ready to serve, stir the cranberries or raisins into the heated fruit. Sprinkle the toasted coconut and nuts over the fruit salad on a small or dessert plate.

Nutritional facts

Calories: 151, Carbohydrates: 39 g, Fat: 0.1 g, Protein: 0.7 g

Chapter 8: Vegetables and Sides

8.1 Asparagus Hot Pot

Preparation Time: 5 min

Cooking Time: 9 min

Servings: 6

Ingredients

- 10 oz bags frozen asparagus
- 1 tbsp extra-virgin olive oil
- 1 tbsp lemon juice
- 1 tsp vegan Worcestershire sauce
- 1/4 cup grated Parmesan-style topping

Instructions

Shake the asparagus into the olive oil, lemon juice, and vegan Worcestershire sauce in a medium bowl. Cook the asparagus in the air fryer baking pan for 7 minutes at 360°F. Cook for a further 2 minutes after adding the vegan Parmesan cheese.

Nutritional facts

Calories: 162, Carbohydrates: 12 g, Fat: 13 g, Protein: 8 g

8.2 Asparagus Roasted

Preparation Time: 5 min

Cooking Time: 10 min

Servings: 4

Ingredients

- 1 lb asparagus
- Salt and pepper to taste
- 1/8 tsp dried tarragon, crushed (non-compulsory)
- 2 tsp extra-light olive oil

Instructions

Trim the woody stems from the asparagus and wash them. On a cutting board or baking sheet, arrange the spears. Season with salt, pepper, and tarragon if using. Pour 1 teaspoon of oil over the spears and turn them to coat them evenly. Add up to 1 teaspoon more oil if necessary, rolling as you spray until all spears are lightly coated. Put the spears in the air fryer basket, bending as needed. They do not need to lie flat. Cook for 5 minutes at 390°F. Shake or swirl the basket to spread the vegetables and cook for 4–5 minutes more or until crisp-tender. Keep an eye on the spears, and don't overcook them.

Nutritional facts

Calories: 150, Carbohydrates: 12 g, Fat: 13 g, Protein: 8 g

8.3 Avocado Boats

Preparation Time: 5 min

Cooking Time: 8 min

Servings: 4

Ingredients

- 1 cup frozen white corn
- 1 cup cooked black beans, drained
- 1/4 cup chopped onion
- 1/2 tsp Tex-Mex Seasoning
- 2 tsp lime juice
- salt and pepper to taste
- 2 avocados
- Sriracha sauce

Instructions

Combine the corn, beans, onion, Tex-Mex seasoning, and lime juice in a mixing bowl; season with salt and pepper to taste. Remove the pits from the avocados and cut them in half. Scoop off roughly 1 tablespoon of the flesh from the center of each avocado half. Distribute the corn mixture evenly between the cavities. Cook the avocado half in the air fryer basket for 6–8 minutes so the corn mixture is hot. Top with jalapeño slices and pass the Sriracha sauce at the table to serve.

Nutritional facts

Calories: 437, Carbohydrates: 28 g, Fat: 33 g, Protein: 10 g

8.4 Barbecue Bellas

Preparation Time: 15 min

Cooking Time: 8 min

Servings: 8 Mushrooms

Ingredients

- Oil for mist over
- 8 baby bella mushrooms
- 1/2 cup barbecue sauce
- 1/2 cup diced fresh pineapple

Instructions

Put cooking spray or oil on the air fryer basket. Remove the mushroom caps' stems and discard or store them for another use. Scrape dark gills from the lower part of the caps using a knife. Combine the barbecue sauce and pineapple in a small bowl. Fill the caps with the BBQ pineapple mixture. Place the caps in the prepared air fryer basket and cook for 8 minutes at 375°F.

Nutritional facts

Calories: 162, Carbohydrates: 12 g, Fat: 13 g, Protein: 8 g

8.5 Broccoli-Rice Casserole

Preparation Time: 15 min

Cooking Time: 20 min

Servings: 8

Ingredients

- Oil for mist over
- 16 oz package soft silken tofu
- 1/2 cup vegan Cheddar-style shreds
- 1 tsp salt
- 2 tbsp almond milk
- 12 oz package broccoli, chopped and thawed
- 1 cup cooked rice

Instructions

Spray the air fryer tray with oil or non-stick spray. Combine the tofu, vegan cheese shreds, salt, and milk in a large mixing basin with an electric mixer. Combine the broccoli and rice in a mixing bowl. Fill the previously greased baking pan halfway with the casserole ingredients. Cook for 20 minutes at 360°F.

Nutritional facts

Calories: 140, Carbohydrates: 2 g, Fat: 1 g, Protein: 10 g

8.6 Brussels Sprouts with Walnuts

Preparation Time: 5 min

Cooking Time: 5 min

Servings: 3

Ingredients

- 10 oz package frozen Brussels sprouts, thawed
- 2 tsp olive oil
- 1 tsp maple syrup
- salt and pepper to taste
- 2 tbsp chopped walnuts

Instructions

Split the sprouts lengthwise. Combine the oil and syrup in a small mixing dish. Toss the sprout halves in the oil mixture to combine. Season the sprouts with salt and pepper to taste in the air fryer basket. Cook at 360°F for 5 minutes or until the edges begin to brown. Move the sprouts to the serving dish, sprinkle with the walnuts, and serve immediately.

Nutritional facts

Calories: 45, Carbohydrates: 9 g, Fat: 0.3 g, Protein: 2 g

8.7 Butternut Squash

Preparation Time: 15 min

Cooking Time: 9 min

Servings: 4

Ingredients

- 1 (2 lbs) butternut squash
- 1/4 tsp salt
- 1/4 tsp cinnamon
- 1 tbsp olive oil
- 2 tbsp vegan butter
- 2 tbsp maple syrup
- 1/4 tsp salt
- 1/4 tsp ground ginger
- 1/4 tsp cinnamon

Instructions

Remove the seeds from the squash and cut it into 1/2-inch pieces. Combine the squash cubes with the seasonings in a large mixing basin and swirl to coat thoroughly. Drizzle the olive oil over the squash cubes and swirl to coat evenly. Put the squash in the air fryer basket and cook for 4 minutes at 390°F. Cook for 4–5 minutes more or until the vegetables are soft. After that, transfer to a serving bowl. Place all the sauce ingredients in an air fryer baking pan and cook at 390°F for 30 seconds, or until the vegan butter melts and the other ingredients are heated. Pour the sauce over the squash and stir to combine the ingredients. To coat the squash cubes equally, mix them with the sauce.

Nutritional facts

Calories: 82, Carbohydrates: 17 g, Fat: 2 g, Protein: 2 g

8.8 Beets

Preparation Time: 5 min

Cooking Time: 40 min

Servings: 8

Ingredients

- 3 (2 lbs) beets

Instructions

Remove the leaves but keep the beetroot stalks for 1 inch. Don't remove the root tails. Wash and pat dry the beets before placing them in the air fryer basket. Cook for around 35–40 minutes at 390°F. The size of the beets will determine the cooking time. When the beets have cooled sufficiently to handle, take off the root and stem ends and peel them.

Nutritional facts

Calories: 66, Carbohydrates: 8 g, Fat: 4 g, Protein: 1 g

8.9 Carrot Pudding

Preparation Time: 22 min

Cooking Time: 30 min

Servings: 4

Ingredients

- 12 oz bags of frozen sliced carrots, partially thawed
- 1/2 cup water cooking spray
- 2 tbsp Bob's Red Mill egg replacer
- 4 tbsp plant-based milk
- 1/4 cup maple syrup
- 1 1/2 tsp baking powder
- 1 1/2 tsp vanilla
- 1 tsp cinnamon
- 1 tsp nutmeg
- 2 tbsp all-purpose flour

Instructions

Chop the carrots coarsely and place them in a medium-sized cooking saucepan with the water. Bring the water and carrots to a boil over high heat. Reduce the heat to medium and simmer for 8–10 minutes or until the vegetables are soft. Set aside a baking pan sprayed with nonstick spray. Drain and purée the carrots in a food processor. Transfer to a medium-sized mixing bowl. Combine the egg replacer and plant-based milk in a small mixing dish. Pour the mixture over the carrots, then top with the other ingredients. Beat the ingredients with an electric mixer until smooth. Place the mixture in a baking dish. Cook for 30 minutes at 360°F.

Nutritional facts

Calories: 120, Carbohydrates: 15 g, Fat: 1 g, Protein: 5 g

8.10 Carrots Glazed

Preparation Time: 10 min

Cooking Time: 10 min

Servings: 4

Ingredients

- 2 tsp pure maple syrup
- 1 tsp orange juice
- 1/2 tsp grated orange rind
- 1⁄8 tsp ginger
- 1 lb peeled baby carrots
- 2 tsp olive oil
- 1/4 tsp salt

Instructions

Set aside maple syrup, juice from the orange, grated rind, and ginger in a small bowl. Toss the carrots in the oil and salts to coat thoroughly. Cook for 5 minutes at 390°F. Shake the basket to distribute the carrots and cook for 2–4 more or until tender. Place the carrots in the baking pan of the air fryer. Stir the syrup mixture one more, then pour it over the carrots and toss to coat. Cook for 1 minute at 360°F until thoroughly heated.

Nutritional facts

Calories: 298, Carbohydrates: 49 g, Fat: 12 g, Protein: 2 g

8.11 Coconut-Curry Pineapple

Preparation Time: 15 min

Cooking Time: 20 min

Servings: 8

Ingredients

- 3 3/4 cups fresh pineapple
- oil to spray
- 1 cup unsweetened coconut flakes
- 1 tsp curry powder
- 1 1/2 cups coconut milk

Instructions

Cut the pineapple into 18-inch cubes. Spray the air fryer baking pan with cooking spray or oil. Combine the pineapple chunks, coconut flakes, and curry powder in a large mixing basin. Pour the coconut milk over the pineapple mixture into the air fryer baking tray. Cook for 20 minutes at 360°F.

Nutritional facts

Calories: 328, Carbohydrates: 21 g, Fat: 24 g, Protein: 11 g

8.12 Corn Croquettes

Preparation Time: 10 min

Cooking Time: 18 min

Servings: 4

Ingredients

- 1/4 cup chopped red bell pepper
- 1/4 cup chopped poblano pepper
- Oil for mist over
- 1/2 cup leftover mashed potatoes
- 1 1/2 cups frozen corn kernels
- 1/2 tsp onion powder
- 1/4 tsp ground cumin
- 1⁄8 tsp ground black pepper
- 1/4 tsp salt
- 1/2 cup panko breadcrumbs

Instructions

Mist the chopped peppers in the air fryer baking pan with oil. Cook for 3–4 minutes at 390°F to soften them somewhat. Meanwhile, combine the potatoes, corn, and seasonings in a medium mixing dish. Stir in the cooked peppers to the potato mixture well. Form the vegetable mixture into 16 balls. Roll the balls in breadcrumbs, spritz them with oil, and then set them in the air fryer basket. Cook for 12–14 minutes at 360°F or until the croquettes are golden brown and crispy.

Nutritional facts

Calories: 209, Carbohydrates: 36 g, Fat: 7 g, Protein: 7 g

8.13 Fingerling Potatoes

Preparation Time: 5 min

Cooking Time: 18 min

Servings: 4

Ingredients

- 1 lb fingerling potatoes
- 2 tbsp nutritional yeast
- 2 tsp lemon pepper seasoning
- 2 tbsp light olive oil
- Salt to taste

Instructions

Half the potatoes lengthwise. Mix the potatoes, yeast, and lemon pepper in a large bowl. Stir to distribute the seasonings evenly. Stir in the oil to fully coat the potatoes. Place the potatoes in the air fryer basket and cook for 12–18 minutes until lightly browned and soft on the interior. Before serving, taste and season with salt if necessary.

Nutritional facts

Calories: 370, Carbohydrates: 49 g, Fat: 16 g, Protein: 5 g

8.14 French Fries

Preparation Time: 10 min

Cooking Time: 25 min

Servings: 4

Ingredients

- 2 cups fresh potatoes
- 2 tsp light olive oil
- 1/2 tsp salt

Instructions

Slice the potatoes into 1/2-inch pieces. Cut each slice into 1/2-inch fries. Rinse and pat dry the raw fries with a clean towel. Combine the fries, oil, and salt in a plastic bag or a container with a lid. Shake well to combine and coat evenly. Fill the air fryer basket halfway with fries. Cook for 10 minutes at 390°F. Shake the basket to disperse the fries and cook for another 15 minutes, until golden brown.

Nutritional facts

Calories: 370, Carbohydrates: 49 g, Fat: 16 g, Protein: 5 g

8.15 Green Beans Sesame

Preparation Time: 10 min

Cooking Time: 22 min

Servings: 4

Ingredients

- 1 lb fresh green beans
- 1 tbsp sesame oil
- 1/2 onion, julienned
- 1 tbsp sesame seeds
- 1/4 tsp crushed red pepper flakes
- Oil for mist over
- 1 tbsp soy sauce

Instructions

Clean the beans and cut the stem ends off. Toss the beans with the oil from the sesame seeds in a large mixing dish. Put them in the air fryer basket and cook for 5 minutes at 330°F. Cook for 5 minutes more after shaking the basket. Cook for another 2–4 minutes or until the beans are cooked to your liking. They may shrivel and become brown in spots. Set aside after removing from the basket. Place the slivered onion in the baking pan of the air fryer. Mist with oil after stirring in the sesame seeds and red pepper. Cook for 5 minutes in the oven. Cook for 2–3 minutes more, stirring occasionally, until the onion is crisp-tender. Combine the onions and soy sauce in a mixing bowl. Pour the onion mixture over the green beans and mix thoroughly.

Nutritional facts

Calories: 120, Carbohydrates: 7 g, Fat: 8 g, Protein: 4 g

8.16 Hasselbacks

Preparation Time: 10 min

Cooking Time: 41 min

Servings: 4

Ingredients

- 2 (1 lb each) potatoes
- Oil for mist over
- Salt and pepper to taste
- Garlic powder
- 1 1/2 oz vegan Cheddar-style shreds
- 1/4 cup chopped green onion tops
- Vegan sour cream (non-compulsory)

Instructions

Preheat the air fryer to 390°F. Clean the potatoes and cut them crosswise every 14–12 inches, about 34 inches through. You want the potato's bottom to stay intact. Mist the potatoes with oil after fanning them gently to separate the pieces. Season the slices using salt, pepper, and garlic powder to taste. As raw potatoes do not bend easily, massage some oil and seasonings between the slices. Cook for 40 minutes, or until the potatoes test is done when probed with a fork, in the air fryer basket. Sprinkle vegan Cheddar-style shreds over the potatoes, pressing some down among the pieces. Cook for 30–60 seconds more to soften the vegan Cheddar-style shreds. Cut each potato in half crosswise, top with green onions, and serve warm. If desired, top with vegan sour cream.

Nutritional facts

Calories: 213, Carbohydrates: 21 g, Fat: 9 g, Protein: 13 g

8.17 Home Fries

Preparation Time: 8 min

Cooking Time: 25 min

Servings: 4

Ingredients

- 3 lbs potatoes
- 1/2 tsp olive oil
- Salt and pepper to taste

Instructions

Cut potatoes into 1-inch chunks. Stir the potatoes and oil together in a large mixing basin to coat completely. Place the potatoes in the air fryer basket and cook for 10 minutes at 390°F. Shake the basket to redistribute the home fries and cook for 10–15 minutes, or until the potatoes are brown and crisp. Season to taste with salt and pepper.

Nutritional facts

Calories: 370, Carbohydrates: 49 g, Fat: 16 g, Protein: 5 g

8.18 Mushroom Sauté

Preparation Time: 5 min

Cooking Time: 5 min

Servings: 4

Ingredients

- 8 oz sliced white mushrooms
- 1/4 tsp garlic powder
- 1 tbsp vegan Worcestershire sauce

Instructions

Rinse and drain the mushrooms thoroughly. Combine the mushrooms in a large mixing bowl and season with garlic powder and vegan Worcestershire sauce. Stir thoroughly to ensure equitable distribution. Put the mushrooms in the air fryer basket and cook at 390°F for 4–5 minutes or until soft.

Nutritional facts

Calories: 60, Carbohydrates: 5 g, Fat: 3.5 g, Protein: 3 g

8.19 Mushrooms Battered

Preparation Time: 10 min

Cooking Time: 12 min

Servings: 4

Ingredients

- 1 tbsp Bob's Red Mill egg replacer
- 2 tbsp water
- 8 oz whole white button mushrooms
- 1/2 tsp salt
- 1/8 tsp pepper
- 1/4 tsp garlic powder
- 5 tbsp potato starch
- 2 tbsp almond milk
- 1 cup breadcrumbs
- Cooking spray

Instructions

Whisk together the egg replacer and water in a small bowl and set away to thicken. Spread the breadcrumbs out on a platter or shallow dish. Combine the mushrooms, salt, pepper, and garlic powder in a large mixing bowl, and toss well to distribute the flavors properly. Toss the mushrooms in the potato starch to coat well. Whisk the almond milk into the egg mixture until completely combined. Roll the mushrooms in the breadcrumbs after dipping them in the milk mixture. Place the breaded mushrooms in the air fryer basket and spray them with oil. It is okay if you have to crowd them, and you may have to stack a few of them. Cook for 5 minutes at 390°F. To reorder the mushrooms, shake the basket. If you notice any white areas, spray them with oil. Cook for 5–7 minutes more or until the mushrooms are golden brown and crispy.

Nutritional facts

Calories: 60, Carbohydrates: 5 g, Fat: 3.5 g, Protein: 3 g

8.20 Mushrooms in Soy

Preparation Time: 5 min

Cooking Time: 5 min

Servings: 4

Ingredients

- 8 oz sliced white mushrooms
- 1/4 tsp dried rosemary
- 1/4 tsp dried thyme
- 1 tbsp soy sauce

Instructions

Place the mushrooms in a large mixing bowl once they have been rinsed and drained. Season the mushrooms with rosemary, thyme, and soy sauce to taste. Stir well to distribute seasonings thoroughly. Cook the mushrooms in the air fryer basket for 4–5 minutes or until soft.

Nutritional facts

Calories: 70, Carbohydrates: 7 g, Fat: 4 g, Protein: 4 g

8.21 Mushrooms Stuffed

Preparation Time: 30 min

Cooking Time: 10 min

Servings: 6

Ingredients

- 8 oz mushrooms
- 1 cup breadcrumbs
- 1 tsp red pepper flakes
- 1 tsp ground allspice
- 1 tsp thyme
- 4 tbsp extra-virgin olive oil
- Oil for mist over

Instructions

Cut the stems from the mushrooms, chop them, and place them in a medium mixing bowl. Remove the dark gills off the mushroom caps inside using a knife's tip. Place the caps, gill side down, on a piece of wax paper. Mix the breadcrumbs, red pepper flakes, allspice, thyme, and olive oil into the minced stems. Oil the caps and flip them over, gill side up. Form the filling into the same number of balls as mushroom caps. After pressing the balls into the caps, place the stuffed caps in the air fryer basket. If you position them close together, you can accommodate them in a single layer. If not, they can be stacked. Cook for 10 minutes at 360°F to heat through.

Nutritional facts

Calories: 60, Carbohydrates: 5 g, Fat: 3.5 g, Protein: 3 g

8.22 Okra and Tomatoes

Preparation Time: 10 min

Cooking Time: 25 min

Servings: 4

Ingredients

- 1 lb fresh okra
- 15 oz can stewed tomatoes
- 1/4 cup mirepoix

Instructions

Remove the stem ends of the okra and trash it or save it for another use. Place the okra pods in the air fryer baking tray, cut into 14-inch slices. Over the okra, sprinkle the mirepoix. Pour the cooked tomatoes over the okra, including the liquid. Cook for 20–25 minutes at 390°F or until the okra is soft.

Nutritional facts

Calories: 113, Carbohydrates: 16 g, Fat: 1.2 g, Protein: 1.9 g

8.23 Okra Battered

Preparation Time: 15 min

Cooking Time: 15 min

Servings: 4

Ingredients

- 1 tablespoon Bob's Red Mill egg replacer

- 1 cup almond milk
- 8 oz fresh okra
- 1 cup plain breadcrumbs
- 1/2 tsp salt
- Cooking spray

Instructions

Set aside the egg replacer and milk in a large mixing dish. Remove the okra stem ends and discard or save them for another use. Cut the okra pods into 12-inch pieces crosswise. Stir the okra slices into the milk mixture to coat. Combine the breadcrumbs and salt in a plastic bag or a container with a cover. Take the okra from the egg mixture with a slotted spoon, allowing the excess to drip off, and place the slices in the bag or container with breadcrumbs. Remove a few okra slices at a time to enable sufficient egg wash to run off. Drain the okra thoroughly before coating it in breadcrumbs. Coat the okra in the crumbs well. Fill the air fryer basket halfway with coated okra and drizzle with oil or cooking spray. The okra does not have to fit in a single layer, nor do you have to spray both sides at this point. A good spray on top will be enough. Cook for 5 minutes at 390°F. Shake the basket to reorganize the okra and spray with oil while shaking. Cook for 5 minutes more. Shake and re-spray to cover any white places you may have missed. Cook for another 2–5 minutes, or until the okra is golden brown and crispy.

Nutritional facts

Calories: 152, Carbohydrates: 18 g, Fat: 4 g, Protein: 4 g

8.24 Onion Rings

Preparation Time: 15 min

Cooking Time: 14 min

Servings: 4

Ingredients

- 1 onion
- 1/2 cup all-purpose white flour
- 1/2 tsp salt

- 1/2 cup beer, plus 2 tbsp
- 1 cup crushed breadcrumbs
- Cooking spray

Instructions

Cut the onion crosswise into rings. Combine the flour and salt in a large mixing bowl. Pour the beer slowly over the flour mixture. Stir until it stops bubbling and becomes a thick batter. Stir a few onion rings in the sauce to coat them thoroughly. Place the breadcrumbs in a plastic bag or a container with a cover. Working in batches, take the onion rings from the batter, brush off the excess, and place them in the breadcrumbs. Shake the bag or container to coat the onions, then spread them on a baking sheet or wax paper. After you've breaded all the rings, brush both sides with oil and place them into the air fryer basket. Cook for 5 minutes at 390°F. Shake the basket, re-spray the rings with oil, and cook for 5 minutes more. Mist again and cook for another 2–4 minutes or until the rings are golden brown and crispy.

Nutritional facts

Calories: 140, Carbohydrates: 2 g, Fat: 1 g, Protein: 10 g

8.25 Peas with Mint and Lemon

Preparation Time: 5 min

Cooking Time: 5 min

Servings: 4

Ingredients

- 10 oz package of frozen green peas, thawed
- 1/2 tsp grated lemon zest
- 1 tbsp fresh mint, shredded (non-compulsory)
- 1 tsp melted vegan butter

Instructions

Toss the peas, lemon zest, mint (if used), and warmed butter together. Put the peas into the air fryer basket and cook at 360°F for 5 minutes or until the peas are heated.

Nutritional facts Onion Rings

Calories: 60, Carbohydrates: 5 g, Fat: 3.5 g, Protein: 3 g

8.26 Peas with Mushrooms and Tarragon

Preparation Time: 15 min

Cooking Time: 10 min

Servings: 4

Ingredients

- 1/2 cup vegetable broth
- 2 1/2 cups fresh green peas
- 1 cup finely diced mushrooms
- 1/2 cup thinly sliced green onions
- 1 1/2 tsp dried tarragon
- 1/2 tsp salt

Instructions

In a medium bowl, stir the peas, garlic, mushrooms, onions, tarragon, and salt into the vegetable broth. Fill the air fryer baking pan halfway with the mushroom mixture. Cook for 5 minutes at 360°F. Cook for 5 minutes more, stirring occasionally.

Nutritional facts

Calories: 70, Carbohydrates: 7 g, Fat: 3.5 g, Protein: 3 g

8.27 Potato Logs

Preparation Time: 5 min

Cooking Time: 15 min

Servings: 4

Ingredients

- 1 lb Gold potatoes
- 3/4 cup dry breadcrumbs
- 1/2 tsp garlic powder
- 1/2 tsp salt
- Oil for mist over

Instructions

To prevent browning, cut the potatoes crosswise into thick wedges, putting them in a water bowl as you go. Combine the breadcrumbs, garlic powder, and salt on a shallow plate. Remove the potatoes from the water, one at a time, without drying them, and roll them in the breadcrumb mix. Coat the potato logs in cooking spray and place them in the air fryer basket. The potatoes do not have to be arranged in a single layer. Cook for 8 minutes at 390°F. Shake the basket and heat for 2–7 minutes more, or until the coating is crunchy while the potatoes are cooked through.

Nutritional facts

Calories: 370, Carbohydrates: 49 g, Fat: 16 g, Protein: 5 g

8.28 Ratatouille

Preparation Time: 20 min

Cooking Time: 20 min

Servings: 3

Ingredients

- 1 1/2 cups diced zucchini
- 1 1/2 cups diced yellow crookneck squash
- 1/2 cup diced bell peppers
- 1/2 cup diced onion
- 1–3 minced garlic cloves
- 1 tbsp extra-virgin olive oil
- 1 tbsp Tuscan Herb Mix
- 1/2 tsp salt
- 8 cherry tomatoes

Instructions

Toss the zucchini, squash, bell pepper, onion, and garlic with the oil, Tuscan Herb Mix, and salt until thoroughly coated. Fill the air fryer baking pan halfway with the veggie mixture. Cook for 10 minutes at 390°F. Add the cherry tomatoes and stir to combine. Cook for 10 minutes more, stirring occasionally, before serving.

Nutritional facts

Calories: 153, Carbohydrates: 21 g, Fat: 7 g, Protein: 4 g

8.29 Root Vegetables

Preparation Time: 10 min

Cooking Time: 20 min

Servings: 4

Ingredients

- 2 tbsp vegetable broth
- 2 cups small red potatoes
- 2 cups baby carrots
- 2 cloves garlic
- 1 cup slivered onion
- 1 tbsp light olive oil

Instructions

Cut the potatoes into quarters, the carrots lengthwise and the garlic minced. Combine all ingredients with the vegetable broth in a medium mixing bowl, whisk to coat evenly. Place the vegetables in the air fryer basket and cook at 360°F for 15–20 minutes or until tender.

Nutritional facts

Calories: 165, Carbohydrates: 28 g, Fat: 7 g, Protein: 2 g

8.30 Squash Casserole

Preparation Time: 20 min

Cooking Time: 35 min

Servings: 4

Ingredients

- 2 (1/4-inch thick) cups shared crookneck squash
- 1 tbsp diced bell pepper
- 1 tbsp onion, minced
- 2 tbsp chopped ripe black olives
- 1 cup breadcrumbs
- 1/2 tsp salt
- 1/4 tsp dried thyme
- 1 tsp dried parsley

- 1 tbsp minced celery
- 4 tbsp vegan butter, melted
- Cooking spray

Instructions

Cook the squash slices in a medium pan of boiling water for 15 minutes or until soft. Drain the slices thoroughly and set them in an adequate mixing dish. Stir in the sliced bell pepper, onion, olives, breadcrumbs, salt, thyme, parsley, and celery. Mix in the vegan butter until everything is wet and nicely combined. Spray the air fryer baking pan with oil and cooking spray, then pour in the casserole ingredients, pressing it down to form a smooth top. Cook for 20 minutes at 360°F. When finished, the top should be lightly browned.

Nutritional facts

Calories: 149, Carbohydrates: 25 g, Fat: 6 g, Protein: 2 g

8.31 Squash Chips

Preparation Time: 20 min

Cooking Time: 12 min

Servings: 4

Ingredients

- 1/2 cup almond milk
- 1 1/2 tsp lemon juice
- 2 tbsp Bob's Red Mill egg replacer
- 4 tbsp water
- 2 yellow squash (about 3/4 lb.)
- 1 cup breadcrumbs
- 1/4 cup white cornmeal
- 1/2 tsp salt
- Cooking spray
- Black pepper

Instructions

Combine the almond milk and lemon juice in a medium mixing dish. Combine the egg replacer and water in a small cup. Cut the squash into 14-inch thick crosswise rounds. Preheat the air fryer to 390°F. Combine 1/4 cup of the breadcrumbs, cornmeal, and salt in

a plastic bag or a container with a cover. Shake well to combine. Put the remaining breadcrumbs in a small bowl. Whisk together the egg mixture and the almond milk in a mixing dish. Stir to coat each of the squash slices with almond milk mixture. Using a slotted spoon, remove the squash slices from the liquid, allowing the excess to drop off, and transfer them to the panko-cornmeal mixture. Shake the bag/container vigorously to coat. Remove the squash slices from the crumb mixture, allowing the excess to fall off again. Stir gently to coat the slices in the almond milk mixture. Add a little more almond milk if you need additional liquid.

Remove the squash slices from the liquid one at a time and dip them into the breadcrumbs in the shallow dish. Place the squash chips in the air fryer basket and coat them with oil or cooking spray. Try to keep them in a single layer, but it's fine if they cluster and overlap in areas. Cook for 5 minutes at 390°F. Shake the basket or use a fork to separate any that have become clumped together. Mist with oil again, cook for 5 minutes more, then recheck the slices. If necessary, spritz with oil again and cook for another 1–2 minutes or until the squash chips are crispy and golden brown. Season generously with freshly ground black pepper

Nutritional facts

Calories: 169, Carbohydrates: 35 g, Fat: 7 g, Protein: 1 g

8.32 Succotash

Preparation Time: 20 min

Cooking Time: 15 min

Servings: 8

Ingredients

- 3 ears corn
- 12 oz package frozen lima beans or butterbeans
- 1/2 tsp garlic powder
- 1/2 cup minced onion
- 1/2 cup almond milk

- Cooking spray

Instructions

Remove the kernels off the cob and shuck the corn. You should have approximately 3 cups of kernels. Combine each of the ingredients in a medium mixing basin. Spray the air fryer baking pan using oil or cooking spray, then add the succotash. Cook for 10 minutes at 360°F. Cook for 5 minutes more, stirring occasionally.

Nutritional facts

Calories: 10, Carbohydrates: 0.3 g, Fat: 1 g, Protein: 0.4 g

8.33 Sweet Potato Home Fries

Preparation Time: 10 min

Cooking Time: 10 min

Servings: 4

Ingredients

- 2 sweet potatoes
- 1 tsp garlic powder
- 1/2 tsp smoked paprika
- 1 tbsp light olive oil
- Oil for mist over
- Salt and pepper to taste

Instructions

Peel the potatoes and cut them into 3–4-inch cubes (peeling is optional). You should have approximately 3 cups of cubes. Combine the potatoes, garlic, and paprika in a large mixing bowl, and whisk thoroughly. Splash the oil on the potatoes and toss to coat evenly. Cook the potatoes in the air frying basket for 5 minutes at 390°F. Rearrange the potatoes by shaking the basket or using a spoon. Mist in oil and cook for another 4–5 minutes or until tender. Season the home fries to taste with salt and pepper.

Nutritional facts

Calories: 170, Carbohydrates: 5 g, Fat: 3 g, Protein: 12 g

8.34 Vegetable Couscous

Preparation Time: 15 min

Cooking Time: 12 min

Servings: 4

Ingredients

- 4 oz fresh mushrooms
- 1/2 green bell pepper
- 1 stalk celery
- 1 cup chopped asparagus
- 1/4 onion
- 1/4 tsp ground coriander
- 1/4 tsp ground cumin
- Salt and pepper to taste
- 1 tbsp light olive oil
- 1 cup vegetable broth
- 3/4 cup uncooked couscous
- 1/2 tsp salt (neglect if consuming salty vegetable broth)

Instructions

Prepare the mushrooms, cut bell pepper into julienne strips, thinly slice the celery, prepare the asparagus, and sliver the onion. Mix each of the vegetables in a large mixing basin. Stir in the coriander, cumin, pepper, and salt to taste, and combine thoroughly. Stir in the olive oil to coat the vegetables evenly. Cook the vegetables in the air basket for the fryer for 5 minutes at 390°F. Cook for 5–7 minutes more or until the vegetables are soft. Meanwhile, bring the broth to a boil in a large saucepan. Cover and take from heat after stirring in the couscous. Allow for a 5-minute rest. Serve the cooked couscous with the prepared vegetables.

Nutritional facts

Calories: 165, Carbohydrates: 28 g, Fat: 7 g, Protein: 2 g

8.35 Zucchini Croquettes

Preparation Time: 10 min

Cooking Time: 6 min

Servings: 4

Ingredients

- Cooking spray
- 2 cups shredded zucchini
- 1/2 cup leftover mashed potatoes
- 1/4 tsp garlic powder
- 1/4 tsp salt
- 2 tbsp potato starch
- 1/2 cup panko breadcrumbs

Instructions

Mist the air fryer baking pan with cooking spray or oil. Cook the shredded zucchini for 3 minutes at 390°F. Cook for 3 minutes more, stirring occasionally, to soften the zucchini. Combine the cooked zucchini, mashed potatoes, garlic powder, salt, and 1 tablespoon of potato starch in a large mixing dish. Stir together. Process half of the veggie mixture in a food processor for about 1 minute, or only enough time to make the mixture very smooth. Stir the processed mixture back into the remaining zucchini-potato mixture. If the mix appears too liquid, add the remaining tablespoons of potato starch. In a small dish, combine the panko crumbs. Form the veggie mixture into 12 balls and roll each one in panko crumbs. Place the croquettes in the air fryer basket and cook at 390°F for 11–12 minutes or until golden brown and crispy outside.

Nutritional facts

Calories: 120, Carbohydrates: 2 g, Fat: 1 g, Protein: 9 g

Chapter 9: Breads

9.1 Artisan Loaf with Roasted Peppers and Olives

Preparation Time: 25 min

Cooking Time: 25 min

Servings: 8

Ingredients

- 1 1/2 tsp coconut sugar
- 1 cup lukewarm water
- 1 package rapid-rise yeast
- 1 cup whole-grain white wheat flour
- 1/8 tsp salt
- 1 tsp dried basil
- 2 tsp extra-virgin olive oil
- 1/3 cup chopped roasted red peppers
- 1/3 cup olives
- Cooking spray

Instructions

In a medium mixing dish, combine the coconut sugar and lukewarm water. Incorporate the yeast. Beat with the flour, salt, basil, then olive oil using a wooden spoon for a total of 2 minutes. Combine the peppers and olives in a mixing bowl. Instead of a hard dough, you will end up with a soft dough. At this time, the batter is thick. Spray or spritz the air fryer baking pan using oil, pour in the batter, and bake for 20 minutes. Smooth out the top. Allow for a 15-minute rise in the batter. Preheat the air fryer to 360°F. Cook the bread for 20–25 minutes or until a toothpick inserted in the center comes out clean. The bread's middle emerges and has moist crumbs clinging to it. Allow the bread to rest in the pan for 10 minutes before removing it.

Nutritional facts

Calories: 774, Carbohydrates: 151 g, Fat: 7 g, Protein: 25 g

9.2 Biscuits

Preparation Time: 10 min

Cooking Time: 9 min

Servings: 4

Ingredients

- 6 tbsp almond milk
- 1 tsp distilled white vinegar
- 1 1/2 cups all-purpose white flour
- 2 tsp baking powder
- 1/4 tsp baking soda
- 1/4 tsp salt
- 3 tbsp cold vegan butter
- Cooking spray
- 1 tsp melted vegan butter

Instructions

Combine the almond milk and vinegar in a small bowl or cup. Preheat the air fryer to 390°F. Mix the flour, baking powder, baking soda, and salt in a medium mixing basin. Cut the cold vegan butter into the flour with a pastry blender. Stir in the almond milk mixture until it forms a stiff dough. Form the dough into 4 1/2-inch thick biscuits. If the dough is too sticky to work with, add an additional tablespoon of flour while shaping. Oil a nonstick cooking spray on the air fryer basket. Place all four biscuits in the basket, brush with melted butter, and bake for 8–9 minutes.

Nutritional facts

Calories: 91, Carbohydrates: 17 g, Fat: 0 g, Protein: 4 g

9.3 Blueberry Muffins

Preparation Time: 15 min

Cooking Time: 10 min

Servings: 8

Ingredients

- 1 1/2 tsp distilled white vinegar
- scant 1/2 cup almond milk
- 1 tbsp flaxseed meal
- 2 tbsp water
- 1 cup all-purpose flour
- 1/4 cup coconut sugar
- 1 tsp baking powder
- 1/2 tsp baking soda
- 1/8 tsp salt
- 2 tbsp coconut oil
- 1/2 tsp pure vanilla extract
- 1/2 cup fresh blueberries
- 8 foil muffin cups
- Cooking spray

Instructions

Add the vinegar to a measuring cup. Fill half a cup with almond milk. Combine the flaxseed meal and water in a small mixing bowl. Preheat the air fryer to 330°F. Combine the flour, sugar, baking powder, baking soda, and salt in a large mixing basin. Heat the coconut oil sufficiently to break it down. Pour it into the basin with the flaxseed meal. Stir in the almond milk and vanilla. Drizzle the liquids over the dry stuff and whisk just until moistened. Do not beat. Carefully fold into the blueberries. Take the liners of 8 foil muffin cups and coat the cups with cooking spray. Distribute the batter among 8 muffin cups and place 4 in the air fryer basket. Cook for 9–10 minutes at 330°F. Repeat with the remaining 4 muffins.

Nutritional facts

Calories: 123, Carbohydrates: 11 g, Fat: 1.5 g, Protein: 15 g

9.4 Bran Muffins

Preparation Time: 10 min

Cooking Time: 11 min

Servings: 8 muffins

Ingredients

- 1 tbsp Bob's Red Mill egg replacer
- 2 tbsp water
- 2/3 cup oat bran
- 1/2 cup all-purpose white flour
- 1 tsp baking powder
- 1/2 tsp baking soda
- 1/8 tsp salt
- 1/4 cup almond milk
- 2 tbsp coconut oil
- 3 tbsp molasses
- 1/2 cup chopped dates
- 8 foil muffin cups

Instructions

Preheat the air fryer to 330°F. Combine the egg substitute and water in a little cup. To thicken, set aside for a minute. In a large bowl, combine oat bran, flour, baking soda, salt, and baking powder. Add the almond milk and coconut oil to another small bowl or saucepan, and reheat it just long enough for the oil to start melting. Blend well after adding the molasses and egg combination. Add the liquid mixture and whisk briefly when the dry ingredients are barely moistened. It should not be beaten. Add the dates gradually. Place 4 foil muffin cups in the air fryer basket without using paper liners. Fill each cup 3/4 full with batter. Cook for 10–11 minutes, or until the toothpick inserted in the center comes out clean and the top springs back when softly pressed. Cook the remaining 4 muffins in the same manner.

Nutritional facts

Calories: 67, Carbohydrates: 12 g, Fat: 2 g, Protein: 1 g

9.5 Carrot-Nut Muffins

Preparation Time: 10 min

Cooking Time: 12 min

Servings: 8 muffins

Ingredients

- 3/4 cup whole wheat flour
- 1/4 cup oat bran
- 2 tbsp flaxseed meal
- 1/4 cup coconut sugar

- 1 tsp baking powder
- 1/4 tsp salt
- 1/2 tsp pumpkin pie spice
- 3/4 cup almond milk
- 2 tbsp Date Paste
- 1/2 tsp pure vanilla extract
- 3/4 cup grated carrots
- 1/2 cup chopped walnuts
- 1 tbsp pumpkin seeds
- 16 foil muffin cups
- Cooking spray

Instructions

Preheat the air fryer to 330°F. Mix the flour, bran, flaxseed meal, sugar, baking soda, salt, and pumpkin pie spice in a bowl. Mix the milk, date paste, and vanilla in a medium basin. Just enough to moisten the dry ingredients, add the milk mixture to the flour mixture and whisk. Do not strike. Add the nuts, seeds, and carrots with a gentle whisk. Remove 16 muffin cups' paper liners and save them for later use. Add 2 more cups to make a total of 8, then coat them with cooking spray. Put 4 foil cups in the air fryer basket, and almost completely fill them with batter. Cook for 10–12 minutes at 330°F or until an inside toothpick comes out clean. Prepare the remaining 4 muffins.

Nutritional facts

Calories: 100, Carbohydrates: 7 g, Fat: 2 g, Protein: 4 g

9.6 Chocolate-Cherry Scones

Preparation Time: 20 min

Cooking Time: 11 min

Servings: 9

Ingredients

- Cooking spray
- 2 cups self-rising flour, divided
- 1/3 cup sugar
- 1/3 cup dried cherries
- 2 oz 70% cocoa dark chocolate
- 1/3 cup sliced almonds (optional)
- 1/4 cup vegan butter or coconut oil

- 1 cup almond milk

Instructions

Put cooking spray or oil in the air fryer basket. Set the air fryer to 360°F of temperature. Mix the sugar and 2 cups of flour in a medium bowl. Snip the cherries and chocolate into the flour using kitchen shears, then whisk to combine. If using, combine the chocolate and cherries with the almonds in a bowl. Incorporate butter or coconut oil into the flour mixture using a fork. Add the milk and stir. Turn out the dough onto a sheet of wax paper, sprinkle with the last 1/4 cup of flour, and cover with wax paper. Gently knead by folding and twisting 6–8 times. Create a 6 x 6-inch square out of the dough. Lay the dough squares in the basket after cutting them into 9 equal pieces. Put them near together, but keep them from touching. Cook for 8–11 minutes at 360°F or until just barely browned.

Nutritional facts

Calories: 91, Carbohydrates: 17 g, Fat: 0 g, Protein: 4 g

9.7 Cinnamon Biscuits

Preparation Time: 12 min

Cooking Time: 11 min

Servings: 8

Ingredients

- 3 tbsp coconut sugar
- 3/4 tsp cinnamon
- 1 1/2 cups all-purpose white flour
- 2 tsp baking powder
- 1/4 tsp baking soda
- 3 tbsp cold vegan butter
- 1/2 cup cold vegan sour cream
- 1 tsp almond milk or water additional almond milk
- 1 tbsp melted vegan butter
- Cooking spray

Instructions

Set the air fryer to 360°F of temperature. Combine the sugar and cinnamon in a large bowl. Put aside two tablespoons for the last sprinkle. Mix the remaining cinnamon sugar with the flour, baking soda, and baking powder. Fold the cold butter into the dry ingredients with a pastry blender. To thicken the sour cream, combine it with 1 teaspoon of milk or water in a small bowl. Add the sour cream and fold it into the dry ingredients when a stiff dough forms. Add up to 1 extra tablespoon of almond milk, 1 teaspoon at a time, if the dough is excessively dry. The dough should feel crumbly yet have been thoroughly combined. Spread the dough out on wax paper and knead it for 30–60 seconds, just long enough to incorporate the last of the dry crumbs. Cut the dough into 8 equal pieces, and then form each piece into a biscuit with a diameter of about 2 inches. Sprinkle the reserved cinnamon sugar over the biscuit tops after liberally brushing them with melted vegan butter. Spray some nonstick cooking spray on the air fryer basket. Place the 8 biscuits in the air fryer basket and cook for 9–11 minutes at 360°F, or until done inside.

Nutritional facts

Calories: 91, Carbohydrates: 17 g, Fat: 0 g, Protein: 4 g

9.8 Cinnamon Pecan Bread

Preparation Time: 25 min

Cooking Time: 25 min

Servings: 8

Ingredients

- 3 tbsp coconut sugar
- 1 cup lukewarm water
- 1/4 oz package rapid-rise yeast
- 1 cup whole-grain white wheat flour
- 2 tsp light olive oil
- 1/2 tsp salt
- 2 tsp cinnamon
- 1/2 cup chopped pecans
- Cooking spray

Instructions

Mix the water and coconut sugar in a medium bowl. Add the yeast and mix. After adding them, stir to combine the flour, oil, salt, and cinnamon. Add the pecans and stir. You won't have a stiff dough, but rather a thick batter. Spray the baking dish for the air fryer, then add the batter. Set aside 15 minutes for rising. Set the air fryer to 360°F of temperature. Cook for 20–25 minutes, or until a toothpick inserted into the middle of the dish emerges with moist crumbs sticking to it.

Nutritional facts

Calories: 300, Carbohydrates: 26 g, Fat: 4 g, Protein: 5 g

9.9 Cranberry Muffins

Preparation Time: 10 min

Cooking Time: 10 min

Servings: 8 muffins

Ingredients

- 1 and 1/2 tsp distilled white vinegar
- Scant 1/2 cup almond milk
- 1 tbsp flaxseed meal
- 2 tbsp water
- 2/3 cup oat bran
- 1/2 cup all-purpose white flour
- 1/4 cup coconut sugar
- 1 tsp baking powder
- 1/2 tsp baking soda
- 1/8 tsp salt
- 2 tbsp extra-light olive oil
- 1/4 cup dried cranberries
- 8 foil muffin cups
- Cooking spray

Instructions

Add vinegar to a measuring cup. Add a half cup of almond milk. Combine the flaxseed meal and water in a small bowl and then set it aside. Preheat the air fryer to 330°F. Mix the oat bran, flour, sugar, baking soda, salt, and baking powder in a sizable basin. Combine the flaxseed water with the almond milk mixture and olive oil. Mix the dry ingredients just enough to combine them after adding the liquid components. Do not strike. Fold the cranberries in gently. The 8 aluminum foil muffin pans must remove their liners before being sprayed with cooking oil. Incorporate the batter into the muffin tins. Place 4 muffin cups in the air fryer basket and cook for 9–10 minutes at 330°F. Continue with the 4 additional muffins.

Nutritional facts

Calories: 131, Carbohydrates: 18 g, Fat: 5 g, Protein: 3 g

9.10 Cranberry-Orange Scones

Preparation Time: 20 min

Cooking Time: 11 min

Servings: 9

Ingredients

- Oil for mist over
- 2 cups whole-grain white wheat flour, divided
- 2 tsp baking powder
- 1/3 cup coconut sugar
- 1/4 cup minced dried cranberries
- 1 tsp grated orange peel
- 1/4 cup coconut oil
- 3/4 cup almond or coconut milk
- 1/4 cup fresh squeezed orange juice

Instructions

Apply cooking spray or oil to the air fryer basket. Set the air fryer to 360°F of temperature. Mix 2 cups of flour, baking powder, coconut sugar, cranberries, and orange peel in a medium basin. Blend the coconut oil with the flour mixture using a fork. Add the milk and orange juice and stir to make a soft dough. Turn out the dough onto a piece of wax paper and sprinkle the final 1/4 cup of flour over it. Gently knead by folding and twisting 6–8 times. Create a 6 x 6-inch square out of the dough. Lay the dough squares in the basket after cutting them into

9 equal pieces. Put them near together, but keep them from touching. Until gently browned, cook for 8–11 minutes.

Nutritional facts

Calories: 260, Carbohydrates: 40 g, Fat: 8 g, Protein: 6 g

9.11 Creamy Chive Biscuits

Preparation Time: 10 min

Cooking Time: 10 min

Servings: 4

Ingredients

- 1 cup self-rising flour
- 1 tsp dried chopped chives
- 1/2 tsp garlic powder
- 2 tbsp cold vegan butter
- 1/2 cup cold vegan sour cream
- 1 tsp almond milk or water
- Cooking spray oil to spray

Instructions

Preheat the air fryer to 330°F. Mix the flour, chives, and garlic in a medium basin. Cut the cold butter into the dry ingredients with a pastry blender. To thin the vegan sour cream, combine it with 1 teaspoon of milk or water in a small bowl. When a stiff dough starts to form, add the sour cream and fold it into the dry ingredients. Add up to 1 more tablespoon of almond milk as necessary, stirring in each spoonful. The dough should feel crumbly yet have been thoroughly combined. Just long enough to incorporate the last of the dry crumbs into the mixture, turn the dough out onto a sheet of wax paper and knead for 30–60 seconds. Create 8 sections of dough, then roll each portion into a biscuit about 2 inches in diameter. Spray some nonstick cooking spray on the air fryer basket. Add all 8 biscuits to the air fryer basket, and cook for 8 minutes. Cook the biscuits for a further 2 minutes or until they are done.

Nutritional facts

Calories: 91, Carbohydrates: 17 g, Fat: 0 g, Protein: 4 g

9.12 Tropical Muffins

Preparation Time: 15 min

Cooking Time: 10 min

Servings: 8 muffins

Ingredients

- 1 tbsp flaxseed meal
- 2 tbsp water
- 4 oz fruit cup pineapple tidbits, with juice
- 2 tbsp flour
- 1 cup and 2 tablespoons coconut sugar
- 1 tsp baking powder
- 1/2 tsp baking soda
- 1/8 tsp salt
- 2 tbsp coconut oil
- 1/2 tsp pure vanilla extract
- 1/4 cup chopped macadamia nuts
- 1/4 cup coconut chips
- 8 foil muffin cups
- Cooking spray

Instructions

In a small bowl, mix the flaxseed meal and water. Set the bowl aside. Pre-heat the air fryer to 330°F. After draining, pineapple juice needs to be stored in a measuring cup. The pineapple pieces should only be softly pressed; do not crush them. Combine the grain, sugar, sodium bicarbonate, baking soda, and salt in a sizable basin. The coconut oil is melted with just the right amount of heat. After mixing 12 cups of water into the pineapple juice that was set aside, pour the mixture into the flaxseed water. Blend the oil and vanilla with the flaxseed juice. After introducing the liquid ingredients, stir the dry components just enough to incorporate them. Avoid striking. Add the nuts, coconut tortillas, and pineapple pieces to the batter and gently fold in. Before applying the cooking spray, remove the liners from eight muffin cups constructed from foil. Pour the batter into the muffin pans. Place 4 muffin cups in the air fryer baskets, and cook for 9–10 minutes. Continue making the remaining 4 muffins.

Nutritional facts

Calories: 131, Carbohydrates: 18 g, Fat: 5 g, Protein: 3 g

Chapter 10: This and That

10.1 Cajun Seasoning Mix

Preparation Time: 5 min

Cooking Time: 5 min

Servings: 3/4 cup

Ingredients

- 3 tbsp paprika
- 2 tbsp cayenne pepper
- 2 tbsp dried oregano
- 2 tbsp garlic powder
- 2 tbsp onion powder
- 2 tbsp thyme

Instructions

Mix all components in a small bowl. Keep it in an airtight package.

Nutritional facts

Calories: 131, Carbohydrates: 5 g, Fat: 5 g, Protein: 16 g

10.2 Croutons

Preparation Time: 10 min

Cooking Time: 6 min

Servings: 2 Cups

Ingredients

- 1 tbsp vegan butter
- 1 tbsp extra-light olive oil
- 1/2 tsp garlic powder (non-compulsory)
- 1 loaf bread, about 8 oz.

Instructions

Cook the butter in a small pan over low heat until it starts to become golden. Add the spice and oil and stir. While you make the bread, set it aside. Cut the bread into 34-inch cubes. Place the bread cubes in a large bowl, drizzle the oil mixture over them, and toss to coat thoroughly.

Place the cubes in the air fryer basket and cook for 3 minutes at 390°F. Cook and stir for 3 minutes more or until the croutons are golden brown and crunchy.

Nutritional facts

Calories: 97, Carbohydrates: 9 g, Fat: 6 g, Protein: 1 g

10.3 Date Paste

Preparation Time: 8 hours

Cooking Time: 8 hours

Servings: 1 and 1/2 cups

Ingredients

- 2 cups dates (approx. 16 oz.)
- 2 cups water

Instructions

Submerge the dates in water for a minimum of 8 hours and up to overnight. Drain the dates, reserving the liquid. Pure the dates in a food processor or blender. Add a small amount of the liquid that was set aside and keep processing until smooth paste forms. As you process, carefully add the liquid. Only 1-2 tablespoons of the reserved liquid will be needed. Keeps for up to 2 weeks in the refrigerator in an airtight container.

Nutritional facts

Calories: 555, Carbohydrates: 90 g, Fat: 15 g, Protein: 23 g

10.4 Guacamole

Preparation Time: 7 min

Cooking Time: 7 min

Servings: 4

Ingredients

- 2 avocados
- 1/4 cup finely minced onion
- 1/4 cup finely minced tomato
- 1 tbsp minced jalapeño
- 1/8 tsp garlic powder
- Salt and pepper to taste

Instructions

Remove the pits from the avocados after cutting them in 1/2 or 1/4s. Slide a spoon between the avocado flesh and peel and lift out to separate the flesh. Mash the avocado flesh in a medium bowl using a fork or potato masher. Mix well before adding the onion, tomato, peppers, and garlic powder. Serve right away after adding salt and pepper to taste.

Nutritional facts

Calories: 97, Carbohydrates: 9 g, Fat: 6 g, Protein: 1 g

10.5 Panko Style Breadcrumbs

Preparation Time: 15 min

Cooking Time: 10 min

Servings: 5 cups

Ingredients

1 of 16 oz Loaf white bread

Instructions

Set the oven to 300°F. Slice the loaf into 1-inch thick. Remove and set aside the crusts. Grate the slices using a hand grater. This can also be done in a blender. Pulse the processor while processing 2–3 slices at a time until the bread is reduced to coarse crumbs. Spread the crumbs out into 2 large cookie or baking sheets. Bake for 5–10 minutes. It might take longer if the bread is fresh and moist, but watch out for browning the crumbs. Place the crumbs in a sealed container after they have totally cooled.

Nutritional facts

Calories: 100, Carbohydrates: 21 g, Fat: 0 g, Protein: 4 g

10.6 Pickled Red Onions

Preparation Time: 10 min

Cooking Time: 15 min

Servings: 4 cups

Ingredients

- 1–2 red onions
- 1 (about 12 oz) bottle red wine vinegar
- 1 tsp dried dill
- 1/2 tsp salt

Instructions

Peel the red onions and cut them into thin slices. Put them in the baking pan for the air fryer. Bring the vinegar, dill, and salt to a boil in a small saucepan while stirring constantly. Cover the slices of onion with boiling vinegar. Cook for 15 minutes at 390°F. Before serving, let onions cool and put any leftovers in the fridge in an airtight container. These last for approximately 4–6 weeks.

Nutritional facts

Calories: 340, Carbohydrates: 33 g, Fat: 17 g, Protein: 12 g

10.7 Pico de Gallo

Preparation Time: 15 min

Cooking Time: 15 min

Servings: 2 Cups

Ingredients

- 3/4 cup diced green
- 2 tbsp diced jalapeño peppers (non-compulsory)
- 3/4 cup tomato
- 3/4 cup onion
- 2 tbsp lime juice
- Salt and pepper to taste

Instructions

Combine the peppers, tomato, and onion in a medium bowl. Add the lime juice and stir. Add pepper and salt to taste.

Nutritional facts

Calories: 17, Carbohydrates: 3.7 g, Fat: 0.1 g, Protein: 0.7 g

10.8 Roasted Garlic

Preparation Time: 5 min

Cooking Time: 15 min

Servings: 1 pod

Ingredients

1 bulb garlic

1/8 tsp virgin olive oil

Instructions

Set the air fryer to 360°F of temperature. To reveal the cloves' tips, cut off the top of the bulb. Top the tips of the garlic cloves with a drizzle of oil. Cook the garlic until it softens and is thoroughly roasted, about 15 minutes.

Nutritional facts

Calories: 32, Carbohydrates: 5 g, Fat: 1 g, Protein: 1 g

10.9 Roasted Mini Peppers

Preparation Time: 11 min

Cooking Time: 15 min

Servings: 8

Ingredients

- 1 lb basket mixed mini peppers, red, yellow, and orange
- 1 tbsp olive oil

Instructions

Remove the seeds from the peppers after washing them and halving them lengthwise. Put them into the air fryer basket after coating them in oil. Cook for 5 minutes at 390°F. Cook for an additional 5 minutes after shaking the bowl to redistribute the peppers. Shake the basket once more, then cook the peppers for a further minute or until the edges start to brown.

Nutritional facts

Calories: 97, Carbohydrates: 9 g, Fat: 6 g, Protein: 1 g

10.10 Tex-Mex Seasoning

Preparation Time: 5 min

Cooking Time: 5 min

Servings: 1/2 cup

Ingredients

- 4 tbsp chili powder
- 2 tbsp onion powder
- 1 tbsp garlic powder
- 1 tbsp ground cumin
- 1 tbsp oregano
- 1 1/2 tsp of black pepper

Instructions

Combine all components, then keep them in an airtight container.

Nutritional facts

Calories: 186, Carbohydrates: 34 g, Fat: 4 g, Protein: 4 g

10.11 Texas Two-Step Dip

Preparation Time: 5 min

Cooking Time: 5 min

Servings: 8

Ingredients

- 1 tomato
- 1/2 red bell pepper
- 1/2 avocado
- 1 (15 oz) can black beans
- 1 (15 oz) can whole kernel white corn
- 3 tbsp Italian salad dressing

Instructions

Chop the avocado, tomato, and bell pepper. After that, drain the beans, rinse them, and then drain the corn. Combine all the ingredients in a large dish before being served.

Nutritional facts

Calories: 131, Carbohydrates: 5 g, Fat: 5 g, Protein: 16 g

10.12 Tuscan Herb Mix

Preparation Time: 10 min

Cooking Time: 10 min

Servings: ¼ cup

Ingredients

- 3 tbsp basil
- 2 tbsp oregano
- 2 tbsp rosemary
- 1 1/2 tsp of marjoram
- 1 tbsp fennel seed
- 1 tbsp garlic powder

Instructions

Add all the ingredients to a food processor and process for between 10–20 seconds. Keep it in an airtight package.

Nutritional facts

Calories: 4, Carbohydrates: 1 g, Fat: 1 g, Protein: 1 g

Chapter 11: Meal Plan for 28 Days

Day 1:

- **Breakfast:** Breakfast Cornbread
- **Lunch:** Bell Peppers Stuffed with Hopping John
- **Dinner:** Meatless Loaf

Day 2:

- **Breakfast:** Donut Bites
- **Lunch:** Black Bean Burgers
- **Dinner:** Mini Pizzas

Day 3:

- **Breakfast:** English Muffin Breakfast Sandwich
- **Lunch:** Bread Pockets
- **Dinner:** Mushroom-Onion Hand Pies

Day 4:

- **Breakfast:** Flourless Oat Muffins
- **Lunch:** Brown Rice Bake
- **Dinner:** Pecan-Crusted Eggplant

Day 5:

- **Breakfast:** Lemon-Blueberry Crepes
- **Lunch:** Burritos
- **Dinner:** Poblano Enchiladas

Day 6:

- **Breakfast:** Oatmeal Bars
- **Lunch:** Aloo Patties
- **Dinner:** Polenta 1/2-Moons with Creole Sauce

Day 7:

- **Breakfast:** Peanut Butter Breakfast Sticks
- **Lunch:** Mixed Vegetable Patties
- **Dinner:** Savory Corn Muffins

Day 8:

- **Breakfast:** Portabella Bacon
- **Lunch:** Chickenless Parmesan
- **Dinner:** Seitan Nuggets

Day 9:

- **Breakfast:** Strawberry Jam
- **Lunch:** Chiles Rellenos
- **Dinner:** Sweet Potato Empanadas

Day 10:

- **Breakfast:** Sweet Potato Toast
- **Lunch:** Coconut Tofu
- **Dinner:** Tofu in Hoisin Sauce

Day 11:

- **Breakfast:** Taquitos and Jam
- **Lunch:** Empanadas
- **Dinner:** Tofu Sticks with Sweet and Sour Sauce

Day 12:

- **Breakfast:** Veggie Sausage Corn Muffins
- **Lunch:** Fishless Sticks with Remoulade
- **Dinner:** Vegetable Turnovers

Day 13:

- **Breakfast:** Toast, Plain and Simple
- **Lunch:** Italian Pita Pockets
- **Dinner:** Italian Eggplant Stew

Day 14:

- **Breakfast:** Breakfast Cornbread
- **Lunch:** Mushroom Galette
- **Dinner:** Rutabaga and Cherry Tomatoes Mix

Day 15:

- **Breakfast:** Donut Bites
- **Lunch:** Balsamic Artichokes
- **Dinner:** Garlic Tomatoes

Day 16:

- **Breakfast:** English Muffin Breakfast Sandwich
- **Lunch:** Black gram galette
- **Dinner:** Vegetable Dumplings

Day 17:

- **Breakfast:** Flourless Oat Muffins
- **Lunch:** Stuffed Eggplant Baskets
- **Dinner:** Zucchini Noodles Delight

Day 18:

- **Breakfast:** Lemon-Blueberry Crepes
- **Lunch:** Mujadarra
- **Dinner:** Simple Tomatoes and Bell Pepper Sauce

Day 19:

- **Breakfast**: Oatmeal Bars
- **Lunch:** Brussels Sprouts and Tomatoes Mix
- **Dinner:** Cherry Tomatoes Skewers

Day 20:

- **Breakfast:** Peanut Butter Breakfast Sticks
- **Lunch:** Pumpkin Lentil Curry
- **Dinner:** Delicious Portobello Mushrooms

Day 21:

- **Breakfast**: Portabella Bacon
- **Lunch:** Brussels Sprouts
- **Dinner:** Stuffed Poblano Peppers

Day 22:

- **Breakfast:** Strawberry Jam
- **Lunch:** Spicy Cabbage
- **Dinner:** Stuffed Baby Peppers

Day 23:

- **Breakfast:** Sweet Potato Toast
- **Lunch:** Sweet Baby Carrots Dish
- **Dinner:** Eggplant and Garlic Sauce

Day 24:

- **Breakfast:** Taquitos and Jam
- **Lunch:** Collard Greens Mix
- **Dinner:** Eggplant Hash

Day 25:

- **Breakfast:** Toast, Plain and Simple
- **Lunch:** Crispy Chinese Eggplant with Soy Honey Sauce
- **Dinner:** Sweet Potatoes Mix

Day 26:

- **Breakfast:** Veggie Sausage Corn Muffins
- **Lunch:** Herbed Eggplant and Zucchini Mix
- **Dinner:** Greek Potato Mix

Day 27:

- **Breakfast:** Breakfast Cornbread
- **Lunch:** Flavored Fennel
- **Dinner:** Broccoli Hash

Day 28:

- **Breakfast:** Donut Bites
- **Lunch:** Okra and Corn Salad
- **Dinner:** Air Fried Asparagus

Conclusion

Let's be real here. Eating a balanced diet rich in all the required nutrients gives us the best opportunity to have a functioning metabolism and lead an effective lifestyle. Many people think the Plant-Based Air Fryer diet is only for people who wish to reduce weight. You'll see that it's actually the other way around. This diet offers dietary information that reduces or completely removes your risk of developing heart disease. But even a simplified version of this—choosing meals intentionally high in good fats and low in carbohydrates—is adequate. You may use air fryers to cook crispy dishes with very little fat because air frying is healthier. Food cooked in an air fryer quickly develops a crisp exterior and excellent texture.

Thank you for reading this book. We hope you now have enough information to start. Don't be reluctant to start. Your health and well-being will increase the sooner you begin this diet. We also hope that you will try every wholesome recipe in this book. The next step is to experiment with different recipes. Enjoy the journey!

Made in the USA
Las Vegas, NV
01 November 2023

80011654R00059